edutopia ®

edutopia

Success Stories for Learning in the Digital Age

Foreword by George Lucas

THE GEORGE LUCAS EDUCATIONAL FOUNDATION

MILTON CHEN, EXECUTIVE EDITOR

SARA ARMSTRONG, EDITOR

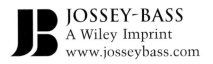

JOSSEY-BASS
A Wiley Imprint
www.josseybass.com

Copyright information continued on page 293.

Published by Jossey-Bass
A Wiley Imprint
989 Market Street, San Francisco, CA 94103-1741   www.josseybass.com

Jossey-Bass books and products are available through most bookstores. To contact Jossey-Bass directly call our Customer Care Department within the U.S. at 800-956-7739, outside the U.S. at 317-572-3986, or fax 317-572-4002.

Jossey-Bass also publishes its books in a variety of electronic formats. Some content that appears in print may not be available in electronic books.

Interior design by Yvo.

Library of Congress Cataloging-in-Publication Data

Edutopia : success stories for learning in the digital age /
The George Lucas Educational Foundation ; foreword by George Lucas ;
Milton Chen, Sara Armstrong, editors.—1st ed.
     p. cm.
Includes index.
 ISBN 0-7879-6082-9 (alk. paper)
 1. School improvement programs—United States—Case studies.
2. Educational innovations—United States—Case studies. 3.
Computer-assisted instruction—United States—Case studies. 4.
Internet in education—United States—Case studies. I. Chen, Milton.
II. Armstrong, Sara. III. The George Lucas Educational
Foundation.
 LB2822.82 .E393 2002
 371.33'4—dc21

2001007993

Printed in the United States of America
FIRST EDITION
PB Printing   10 9 8 7 6 5 4

CONTENTS

ACKNOWLEDGMENTS

This book and DVD project has enabled us to "practice what we preach" about the value of project-based learning for students. It was an ambitious and complex project. It required us to work in teams with others in our organization, with each team member making an important contribution. We sought the expertise of others beyond our own walls. And we used digital technology to create, edit, and produce the words and images of this final product.

So we have many to thank. Our deepest appreciation goes first to the many contributors who provided articles, and the schools, educators, parents, and community groups whose work is reflected in them and the companion DVD. It has been an honor to shine a spotlight on such exemplary and inspiring work in our nation's classrooms.

At our Foundation, all of our staff contributed to some aspect of this project—writing and editing articles, selecting photos, communicating with other writers, producing video for the DVD, handling promotion, fact-checking, and many other tasks. We express our ongoing appreciation to our talented staff colleagues: Geoff Butterfield, Julie Byers, Anais Chakerian, Jen Celoni, Diane Curtis, Diane Demée-Benoit, Ken Ellis, Roberta Furger, Leigh Iacobucci, Carol McCarthy, Sima Mohamadian, Paula Monsef, Mark Sargent, Diana Schneider, Karen Sutherland, Sheila Tuck, Miwa Yokoyama, and Laurie Yusem.

At Jossey-Bass, Lesley Iura, senior editor, and Paul Foster, vice president and publisher, first shared our enthusiasm for the concept of this "multimedia book" and encouraged us to bring it to fruition. The expertise of the Jossey-Bass editorial, design, and marketing teams, including Pamela Berkman, Adrienne Biggs, Jessica Egbert, Elizabeth Forsaith, Christie Hakim, Bruce Lundquist, Currie McLaughlin, Hilary Powers, Elisa Rassen, Yvo Riezebos, and P. J. Campbell and Jeff Penque of their parent company, John Wiley and Sons, has been evident throughout every phase of production.

The *Edutopia* vision originates with the directors of The George Lucas Educational Foundation, innovative leaders from business, nonprofit organizations, and school boards: chairman George Lucas; vice chairman Steve Arnold; Kim Meredith, Kate Nyegaard, Marshall Turner, and Sam Yamada. Our National Advisory Board shares our vision and is invaluable in broadening our perspectives and shaping our content: Linda Darling-Hammond, Stanford University; Carol Edwards, The NEA Foundation for the Improvement of Education; John Gage, Sun Microsystems; Milt Goldberg, National Alliance of Business; Peter Harris, San Francisco 49ers; Sonia Hernandez, Los Angeles County Alliance for Student Achievement; Cindy Johanson, PBS Interactive; Jackie Lain, Standard & Poor's; Barrie Jo Price, University of Alabama; Rob Semper, The Exploratorium; Helen Soulé, Mississippi Department of Education; and Marco Torres, San Fernando High School in Los Angeles.

We express our gratitude—and our admiration—to these many individuals and organizations whose inspiration and perspiration have created the schools our students deserve in this Digital Age. We offer this book and DVD in the hope of creating more of them.

Milton Chen and Sara Armstrong, Editors
The George Lucas Educational Foundation

FOREWORD

See accompanying DVD for related video clip.

GEORGE LUCAS

I've been interested in education for many years now, with vivid memories of my boyhood growing up in Modesto, California. Frankly, I was not very engaged in my classes; in fact, as a boy, I liked to daydream and write stories. I was also interested in philosophical questions. I remember I once asked my mother, "If there is only one God, why are there so many religions?" That question is rich with intellectual possibilities, integrating studies in history, culture, and comparative religion, but that richness was absent from my grade-school textbooks.

In addition to my curiosity about ideas, I also liked to work with my hands, fixing and racing cars. I even thought of being a car mechanic. Outside of school, I learned about the history of automobiles and the economics of the industry. But again I had to find my own way to learn about topics I was passionate about, as my school days were filled with memorizing isolated names and facts.

It took a serious car accident weeks before my high school graduation for me to reconsider my life and chart a new path. I decided to go to college and explore my beginning interests in philosophy, art, photography, and writing. After junior college, when I attended the USC School of Cinema and Television, I found a calling in which I could use my hands and my head, recording and editing pictures and sound, using technology to realize my imagination on the screen. In my own films, and the work of my companies, I have continued to develop technology's ability to transform filmmaking and the entertainment world, much as all of us have seen the benefits of technology in health care, transportation, manufacturing, and many other fields.

Now I'm a parent of three children, and my interest in education has become even more urgent. It's imperative that we create new kinds of schools, freed from an educational system deeply rooted in the distant past and the kinds of schools so many of us attended many decades ago. History dies hard, especially when it involves our schools and our own lives spent in them. Perhaps Dr. Allen Glenn, a professor and former dean of education at the University of Washington, is right when he says, "The biggest obstacle to school change is our memories." Creating schools for the twenty-first century requires less time looking in the rearview mirror and more vision anticipating the road ahead.

My passion for engaging students in deeper learning during the thirteen formative years they spend in schools led me to start a foundation that is now a decade old. I am certain there are many young learners—many more than most of us acknowledge—who, like myself, learn visually as well as verbally, who like to use their hands as well as their heads, and whose creative and artistic talents go untapped in the traditional textbook-based classroom. Granted, in the history of our nation's schools, a decade is not a very long time. But this Digital Decade has brought enormous change to our nation and our world, and has offered up many exciting new possibilities for organizing schools, the curriculum, the professional development of teachers, and the use of digital technologies.

Though it is still in its early stages, the Internet is showing us ways of connecting students and teachers to new sources of knowledge and expertise, such as the impressive collections and curators in our best museums or the creative scientists in our research centers. Such experiences offer the opportunity to break down the traditional isolation of the classroom. Businesses and community groups are developing new partnerships with schools through, for instance, school-to-career projects giving students valuable real-world experiences and helping them see the practical value of their classroom lessons. Teachers are taking on different learning roles, and students in middle school and high school are learning to teach each other and to act in a role formerly reserved only for graduate students: serving as teaching assistants to their own teachers.

This book tells the success stories of schools leading the way to this new future. These stories are not hypothetical, they're actual accounts of courageous pioneers—teachers, principals, superintendents, and educators at all levels—who are blazing trails to a new horizon. They have taken risks, experimented, and in many cases, had to "buck the system." I believe these committed educators are among the most important individuals in our society. By telling their stories, we honor them and their unselfish dedication to the best hope we have for ensuring the future of our democracy: our children.

INTRODUCTION

EDUTOPIA—"THE ACTUAL PROVES THE POSSIBLE"

MILTON CHEN

Edutopia. The word conjures up images of some far-off, unreachable land, where students are motivated to learn, study subjects in depth and over time, and display initiative and independence in organizing their time and work. The quality of their work is astonishing, often several years ahead of current definitions of being "on grade level." Similarly, the teachers are energized by the excitement of teaching. As professionals, they possess strong mastery of their subjects and how to teach them. They have the time and commitment to attend to the academic and social needs of their students as individuals. They regularly plan, analyze, and reflect on their teaching with other teaching colleagues.

These schools do not resemble the bastions that most of us attended, sealed off from contact with the outside community. As Lee Shulman, president of the Carnegie Foundation for the Advancement of Teaching, has observed, "teaching has been an activity undertaken behind closed doors between moderately consenting participants."

Instead, these schools seem more like welcoming community centers, where parents, artists, architects, physicians, and other members of the community flow through the

Portions of this introduction appeared in an article titled "Seeking Edutopia" in *Education Week,* May 16, 2001.

school, contributing their expertise and resources. Technology enables students, teachers, and administrators to reach out beyond the school building. Sources of knowledge and experts as far away as the Library of Congress or NASA are as close as a student's computer screen, offering a window on a genuinely worldwide web of learning possibilities.

Such a vision of powerful teaching and learning is real. It exists today in pockets of innovation around our country. This book and DVD tell the stories of dedicated teachers, administrators, students, and communities that have made "edutopia" a reality across our nation. They have shown what *can* be done, often with the same resources as other schools and sometimes, with fewer. In Immanuel Kant's famous dictum, "The actual proves the possible."

CELEBRATING UNSUNG EDUCATIONAL HEROES

The most precious resources these innovators have are their vision, their daily dedication to providing the best education students deserve, and their ability to persuade others to follow. From principal Tony Bencivenga's commitment to social and emotional learning in his Ridgewood, New Jersey, middle school to Peggy Bryan's courageous stand on bilingual education in her San Jose, California, grade school, these educational pioneers have set out on a different path from the one charted by most public discourse about our schools these days, with its emphasis on high-stakes testing and accountability. They realize that the stakes in that game reward only superficial learning and cannot lead to the types of schools we will need in this century. They understand that there is no such thing as "mandatory education" and that true learning must voluntarily engage students' minds and hearts.

Unfortunately, these extraordinary individuals—and others like them—are largely unsung heroes. By telling their stories of success, imagination, and perseverance, we hope this book and DVD will share the good news in our schools and help others to learn from their examples.

ENGAGING THE PUBLIC THROUGH MEDIA

At The George Lucas Educational Foundation, our mission is to help educators and the larger public envision this brighter future, through our Web site, films, books, videocassettes, DVDs, and CDs. Readers who know our work recognize our belief in the power of technology to fundamentally change the nature of the education enterprise, just as it has done in other fields of business, medicine, manufacturing, and the arts. With schools, it just takes a lot longer.

However, sometimes the progress can be rapid. In our 1997 documentary film *Learn & Live*, we profiled a grade 4–5 class taught by Jim Dieckmann at the Clear View Charter School in Chula Vista, California, not far from the Mexican border. His students were engaged in project-based learning about insects, collecting insect specimens, working in teams to obtain information from the Web, creating multimedia reports, and developing an assessment rubric to evaluate their use of text, images, graphics, and sound.

The class was connected through a fiber-optic cable to San Diego State University, where, through full two-way audio and video, entomologists helped the students examine their insect specimens under an electron microscope. The students' excitement as they prepared to go online with the scientists was palpable. While many fourth graders can barely spell "electron microscope," let alone use one, these students showed us how the traditional curriculum underestimates the speed and depth of learning done by self-motivated students.

AN INTERNET SOLUTION PLACES SCIENTIFIC TOOLS IN STUDENTS' HANDS

Five years later, Jim Dieckmann's classroom still stands as a model. However, some skeptics found it too high-tech and too unique, perhaps too utopian a view. They argued that most schools did not have high-speed cable connections and nearby universities with scientists and electron microscopes. However, just two years later, the Internet provided a solution. In this book, you will find the story of Bugscope, a project of the University of Illinois's Beckman Institute for Advanced Science and Technology, which developed special Web-based software to make an electron microscope available via the Internet to K–12 students anywhere in the country.

That story and others in this book demonstrate how technology is not only providing new forms of content and connectivity but also assisting in transforming human roles and relationships in school systems—perhaps the greater challenge. An analogy can be found in the world of medicine, where the Web has changed the balance of power between patients and physicians, equipping patients with new sources of information to discuss their diagnoses. Similarly, our best schools, in part through technology, are recasting traditional roles and shifting the balance of power between teachers and students.

Now teachers must spend more time as learners, continually sharpening their professional knowledge and craft. Students must take greater responsibility for their own learning—even, at times, tutoring each other. Some schools are taking advantage of students' fluency with technology and placing them in positions as technology teaching assistants, a new and powerful type of teacher-student relationship. Students as productive team members, insightful peer tutors, supportive teaching assistants, and even creative curriculum designers—these are the new roles our students will play in the Digital Age.

EMOTIONAL INTELLIGENCE MORE IMPORTANT THAN IQ

As students work in teams and communicate with each other and manage relationships, they will need well-developed social and emotional skills. These skills will stand them in good stead as they prepare for the digital workplace, where job descriptions are constantly evolving and require "just-in-time learning." Employers are placing greater emphasis on social and communication skills, in addition to the types of technical knowledge required.

This book also profiles how our best schools are emphasizing this undervalued part of the "invisible curriculum," what well-known author Daniel Goleman has called "emotional intelligence." They are showing how "high-tech" needs to be accompanied by "high-touch." Such programs reveal a well-kept secret: emotionally intelligent students often perform better on tests and other measures of learning because they are more equipped to concentrate, persist, and think independently. Only teachers, counselors, and administrators can provide the human nurturing and mentoring needed for students to develop their social and emotional skills. No machine ever will.

THE NEED TO VISUALIZE OUR BEST CLASSROOMS

For these innovations to spread further, educators and parents, as well as business and community leaders, must first see them and understand them. Technology itself can help visualize what these innovations look like at their most basic level—in the classroom, in the words and behaviors of teachers and students. As a Web-based foundation, a dot-org instead of a dot-com, we endeavor to practice what we preach. Our Web site (http://www.edutopia.org) uses the latest in Internet technology to present numerous film segments and expert interviews, as well as related articles and resources, so that users can "see" into these classrooms.

We also acknowledge that the challenges of locating and accessing this content, especially video, from our Web archive remain daunting for many. Our colleagues at Jossey-Bass have been invaluable in helping us assemble this book and DVD as a "best of" collection of our Web content during the past year, along with newly commissioned material. With their encouragement, we have included a DVD with more than an hour of film segments showing the schools and classrooms described in the book, up close and personal.

We hope that this book and DVD pique your interest so that you will want to know more. We have included Web sites for these model projects and a resource list of additional materials. Our Web site contains more short documentary films and interviews, articles, and resources related to the topics addressed here. The three sections of this book mirror the categories of our site: Innovative Classrooms, Involved Communities, and Skillful Educators. The site also includes more extensive "Starting Points" for parents, school board members, university faculty, and members of business and community organizations—the groups whose joint efforts are needed to create our best schools. We invite you to take a closer look at our site.

"THIS COMPUTER IS A PART OF MY BRAIN"

Recently, I met some middle school students who carry laptops in their backpacks. One boy told me how technology should not be a machine you go *to*, but a machine that goes *with you*. He said, somewhat impatiently, "It's a part of my brain. Why would I want to leave it behind in a computer lab?"

These students are young explorers in new educational terrain. Even younger students are standing in tidal marshes and at intersections, using handheld devices to collect and analyze weather and traffic data. Portable computing is already opening up new possibilities for students to learn in and outside of classrooms, and in the nighttime, weekends, and summers as well as by day. And, on the not-too-distant horizon, new technologies promise to deliver swifter access and new forms of multimedia content to our schools, homes, and communities.

These developments will continue to force our human institutions of schools to respond. They raise the most fundamental questions of educational identity and demand more thoughtful answers: What does it mean to be a teacher? How do we define a student? And how should we design our schools? Our best schools are already providing answers to these questions and demonstrating that our students, not our computers, are the most marvelous learning machines. Children are born wired to learn. Their brighter future is now, right in front of us, if we can only grasp it. Welcome to Edutopia!

edutopia®

PART 1

INNOVATIVE CLASSROOMS

Innovative classrooms are abuzz with productive discussion and the excitement of learning. Students are working in teams on challenging projects, asking questions of each other, reviewing each other's work, and referring each other to new sources of information. Their teachers know when to provide direct instruction through a lecture or presentation and when to allow students to discover on their own.

Other adults—parents, business and community volunteers, student teachers, and teacher's aides—are also in the room, assisting student teams and lowering the adult-student ratio in the class. The teams have access to technology of various kinds, enabling them to access worlds of knowledge beyond the classroom, consult with other experts, assemble their work, and share it with their teachers and classmates. They also know that the audience for their work lies beyond their classrooms, in their families, the community, and visitors to their Web site.

The Digital Age redefines the boundaries of the classroom. No longer are students confined to learning within the four walls of a room or the edges of a school campus. The classroom can now be a forest or stream, an office or lab, a museum or a zoo or anywhere real issues present themselves and professionals are working to understand them. Increasingly, the Digital Age is bringing these environments to students virtually, so that students in class or at home can travel via the Internet to a scientist's laboratory or a curator's collection.

Innovative classrooms are not defined by fixed places but by their spirit of curiosity and collaboration among students, teachers, and others in a true learning community.

Project-Based Learning

In project-based learning, students investigate rich and challenging issues and topics, often in the context of real-world problems, integrating subjects such as science, mathematics, history, and the arts. Students typically work in teams, using technology to access current information and, in some cases, consult with experts. They coordinate time and work schedules, develop real work products such as multimedia reports, and present them to their teachers and the larger community, often in a culminating presentation. Concrete, hands-on experiences come together with more abstract, intellectual tasks to explore complex issues.

The stories that follow profile projects in which students use innovative Web sites with rich content and participate in online projects that extend classroom resources. Handheld and laptop computers and assistive technology meet student needs for portability and for fully realizing the capabilities of each student. Classroom practices such as looping, multi-age classroom grouping, and school-to-career programs encourage a different approach to organizing our schools.

These inspiring stories might lead you to consider steps to incorporate their projects and practices in your local schools. Here are some suggestions, for different roles played by three key stakeholder groups in education: parents, educators (including teachers and administrators), and policymakers (such as superintendents, school board members, and legislators). Some of these suggestions imply the roles of others, such as universities and community organizations, as well. Further "action steps" for all of these groups are given on our Web site at http://www.edutopia.org.

What parents can do:

- Become acquainted with project-based learning practices through Web sites or printed material (see the resource list at the end of this book for a starting point).

- Talk with your child's teacher about possible projects and offer your assistance, for example, by locating needed resources such as materials, organizations, or experts, offering your own expertise, or driving students on project-related outings.

- Organize a session at a PTA meeting to discuss the value of project-based learning and how it can be implemented at your school.

What educators can do:

- Locate current projects that your schools or classes can join. (A good place to start is The Global SchoolNet Foundation's Project Registry at http://www.globalschoolnet.org/gsh/pr/).

- Share your project ideas with other educators at faculty meetings and conferences or electronically, through Web sites or via e-mail discussion lists including educators with common interests.

- Commit to implementing at least one in-depth, project-based learning experience in each course or classroom.

What policymakers can do:

- Become familiar with project-based learning as a way of reorganizing schools, locating examples from your geographic area or on topics of interest. Review the research on the effects of project-based learning to improve student achievement and motivation.

- Work with local, state, and national policy committees to include well-developed project-based learning programs in standards and curriculum frameworks. Support funding for materials, technology, professional development of educators, and other factors needed to implement project-based learning.

NASA Initiatives Turn Students into Scientists

MARILYN WALL

My school, John Wayland Elementary, population 620, is located in the Shenandoah Valley of Virginia, a conservative agricultural area. Shopping is still done in small country stores. The busy street in each town is named Main and is crisscrossed by county dirt roads. Mennonite horses and buggies pass our school each day.

Living in such an area, my students often think of their futures in limited terms—working on farms or in poultry houses, driving a truck, or working in a small family-owned business. Stars, planets, and astronomy are topics not usually discussed at the dinner table, certainly not as leading to possible career choices. That is, not until my students and I connected with NASA.

USING THE TOOLS OF SCIENTISTS

I used to be uncomfortable with science, focusing instead on reading, writing, and math.

I became confident in my own ability to conduct scientific investigations.

But about five years ago, I happened to attend a technology conference where teachers described their students' experiences with science through the Internet, and I clicked onto my first Web page—NASA's K–12 Quest Initiative. I heard about students going on a virtual flight aboard the Kuiper Airborne Observatory. And I learned about an upcoming project called "Live From the Stratosphere."

The first "Live From the Stratosphere" telecast included an invitation for students to participate via the Internet in a global star count, and demonstrated how to turn a simple paper towel tube into a "star count" data instrument. Back at school, my students and I followed the directions, made our star counters, and began practicing. The students felt so important using the star counters and protractors. These were the tools of "real scientists"!

SEEING NEW POSSIBILITIES

On the night of our star count, students took their parents outside and instructed them on how to gather star data for NASA. The next morning I listened to students eagerly comparing their data, not only with each other but with other collaborating schools online. I knew I had a room full of successful learners. My students felt like real research scientists as they entered data on a star census map. They had learned to collect, analyze, and share information. I will always remember this activity because it was the turning point for me—the first time I became confident in my own ability to conduct scientific investigations.

As we continued to explore more space projects, parents became curious. So, when NASA scheduled a special overnight observing session for students to link through live video and

Internet connections with the Kuiper Airborne Observatory, we jumped on the opportunity to invite parents for a "star party." When the night arrived and my students came with parents and guests, I saw such a transformation. Fourth graders took on the role of teachers, escorting adults around our room, explaining their infrared light experiments, demonstrating principles of flight with model planes, and showing their star census data. My students then logged on and found themselves face-to-face with a NASA astronomer. Parents were absolutely amazed to watch their children proudly exchange messages with an astronomer at work.

JOSH'S TRANSFORMATION

I have a last story to share. One student, whom I will call Josh, was a nine-year-old boy, a boy forgotten, with little support from home. He came in each day with an unwashed face, rumpled hair, jeans well worn, and duct tape around his shoe to keep it from falling apart.

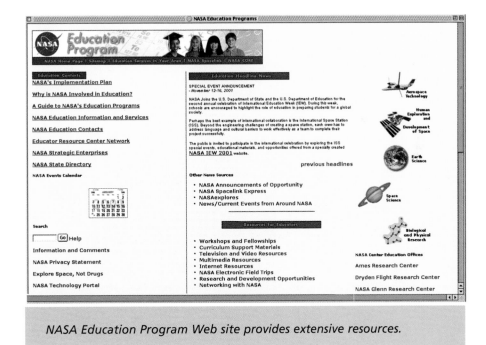

NASA Education Program Web site provides extensive resources.

Josh was reading below grade level and regularly failing to do homework. He needed to wear glasses but absolutely refused to do so.

Slowly, through the course of our projects, Josh began to change. He became eager to work on the computer. Homework assignments started coming in, and Josh began reading "space" books. The night of our star party, I thought Josh would not be able to attend because his mother worked the night shift. But there he was, wearing his glasses, with his mom as his guest! During the telecast, Josh stood beside me and said, "Look at him," and he pointed to a NASA astronomer. Josh pointed again and said, "He wears glasses—just like me."

> Josh came over to me and said, "I'm going to work hard like her."

BUDDING SCIENTISTS

Later that evening, April Whitt, one of the scientists aboard Kuiper, e-mailed my students about how school had not been easy for her, but determination to see "tough things" through got her where she is. Josh came over to me and said, "I'm going to work hard like her." All I could do was hug him and say, "Thank you, NASA scientists!"

For my students in the Shenandoah Valley, technology has become the equalizer, bridging the gap between culturally advantaged urban students and culturally disadvantaged rural students. Though many of my students have never traveled outside our county's borders, never walked through a museum's doors, never looked through a telescope, never felt the ocean waves washing over their feet, never even experienced the moving steps of an escalator or the swaying motion of a train, they have counted stars, shared data with national scientists, participated in live NASA shuttle missions, and perhaps begun to see possibilities for themselves beyond our small part of this fascinating time and space.

Related Web site: education.nasa.gov

INTERNET ACCESS IN EIGHTY-FOUR PERCENT OF AMERICAN CLASSROOMS

The rate of adoption of computers and the Internet in schools continues to accelerate. According to a national survey of schools conducted by Quality Education Data, a research firm in Denver, Colorado, 84 percent of American public school classrooms and 97 percent of schools were connected to the Internet in the fall of 2001. Three years earlier, in 1998, only about one-third of classrooms had Internet access.

The continuing increase in technology access in schools was attributed in part to the impact of $2.25 billion in government funding for the E-rate program, providing discounts to schools for Internet connectivity. The funding has been critical in enabling poorer schools to gain Internet access.

The study also found that the average student-to-computer ratio continued to decrease to 5:1 during the 2000–01 school year. In addition, 22 percent of school districts are providing handheld computers to staff, especially technology coordinators and principals.

Project-Based Learning Online

A Sampler of Projects

DIANE CURTIS AND SARA ARMSTRONG

The following online projects further demonstrate how thoughtful use of the Internet is extending classroom walls for K–12 students. These projects involve the youngest to the oldest students, or a combination of age groups, in researching topics and sharing information in all curriculum areas. Web sites for finding projects include The Global SchoolNet Foundation's Project Registry (http://www.globalschoolhouse.org/pr), Dr. Judi Harris's "Virtual Architecture" Home Page (http://virtual-architecture.wm.edu/), and Dr. Bernie Dodge's WebQuest site (http://webquest.sdsu.edu/webquest.html).

INTERNATIONAL SCHOOLS CYBERFAIR

In 1995 The Global SchoolNet Foundation developed a contest challenging students to "share and unite" with local communities to identify specific information and publish it

through the Internet. Since then, over half a million students from fifteen hundred schools in seventy countries have participated in the International Schools CyberFair. Eight categories (local leaders, businesses, community organizations, historical landmarks, environment, music, art, and local specialties) encourage students to find out about particular people, places, projects, and events. Through working together to develop a school entry to the contest, students deepen their understanding about where they live, build their Web site development skills, and impart meaningful information that would otherwise be unavailable to interested students and adults from around the world. A special feature of the contest is the peer review, in which students evaluate other students' Web sites, providing feedback in a comprehensive online evaluation instrument.
www.globalschoolhouse.org/GSH/cf

GEOGAME

Where in the world are you? Three times a year since 1991, students use atlases, maps, encyclopedias, almanacs, and other tools to identify a city based on a number of clues presented in GeoGame. Developed by Tom Clauset and supported by The Global SchoolNet Foundation, this popular online game encourages map reading, deductive thinking, and collaboration in solving the mystery. Online resources include GeoGame activities, strategies for winning, and archives of previous games.
www.globalschoolnet.org/gsh/project/gg/

GLOBAL SHOPPING LIST

What do peanut butter, milk, sugar, and eggs cost?

How much do peanut butter, milk, sugar, and eggs cost in different states and countries? For thirteen years, students have visited their local marketplaces and collected pricing information, then uploaded it to the Global Shopping List site. The data are available for use in classrooms so that students can compare prices, analyze the information, develop theories for cost differences, and build on what they know. U.S. and world price lists can be viewed on the computer screen or transferred to a spreadsheet. Lesson strategies for using the data can also be found on the Web site.

http://landmark-project.com/ggl/index.html

THE HOLOCAUST/GENOCIDE PROJECT FROM IEARN

Sponsored by iEARN (The International Education and Resource Network) for a decade, the Holocaust/Genocide Project has been bringing together students from around the world to research, discuss, and share their thoughts, writing, and art work through a yearly international magazine, *An End to Intolerance,* as well as online forums and e-mail exchanges. Designed for students aged twelve and up, the project is interdisciplinary, including history, current events, language arts, fine art, foreign languages, and critical thinking. One of many iEARN projects—which currently involve over four hundred thousand participants from nearly a hundred countries in twenty-nine languages—the Holocaust/Genocide Project enables students to learn more about themselves and others as they develop into global citizens.

www.iearn.org

JASON PROJECT

After oceanographer Bob Ballard discovered the wreck of the *Titanic* in 1986, he founded the JASON Project to capitalize on the excitement students around the world felt about the venerable ocean liner. Named after the mythical Greek hero, the JASON Project sponsors yearly expeditions and provides curriculum, professional development programs for teachers, and online networks connecting students, educators, and scientists. One year the expedition goes to forests, including tropical rainforests; the next on an underwater voyage to study how life adapts to a changing sea. Eight to twenty student "Argonauts"

Students perform experiments to extend their JASON Project learning.

and their teacher are chosen to accompany Ballard and other scientists, but most Argonauts take the voyage through live, interactive broadcasts from sites using advanced technologies in robotics, fiber optics, television production, computer science, mechanical and electrical engineering, and satellite communications. Students in these participating classrooms have opportunities to question the on-site participants. The curriculum includes interdisciplinary assignments such as reading novels that pertain to the expedition, integrating art, making personal connections with host researchers, and researching the geography, history, and culture of a project.

www.jason.org

JOURNEY NORTH

Through e-mail and the Internet, Journey North makes scientists of thousands of North American schoolchildren who create a comprehensive picture of the migratory path of Monarch butterflies and other species through individual observations. Students spotting Monarchs in New York can enter their data into the Journey North databank and compare them with other student observations as the Monarchs make their 2,500-mile spring journey from Mexico to Canada. By recording the migration and noting changes in daylight, temperatures, and other conditions, the students create a digital map of the migration as it occurs. More than six thousand schools are involved in the program, which tracks the journeys of a dozen migratory species and records data on other signs of spring, such as blooming periods for tulips in different parts of the country. The program, which also includes a Journey South segment, offers live, interactive programming with professional scientists as well as satellite coverage of the migrations.

www.learner.org/north

SPACE DAY

Once a year, a group of famous astronauts and other luminaries gathers at the Smithsonian's National Air and Space Museum to take part in Space Day, a "salute to the achievements,

Students confer with an astronaut during Space Day activities.

benefits, and opportunities in the exploration and use of space." On that day, the Museum attracts many students and adults interested in the awe-inspiring accomplishments of space travel, but a far greater number are glued to their computers for a live, interactive Webcast, the culminating event of a year of space-related school activities. Each year, Space Day officials issue a design challenge to students, such as developing a nutritious menu for astronauts or a plan for emergency survival. During Space Day, many of the team designs are presented. Via the Web, students pose questions to such heroes as former astronauts Senator John Glenn and Dr. Sally Ride. They participate in live polls, take quizzes on space, and exchange messages with other online users. The Space Day Web site offers a wealth of ideas for classroom projects, easy-to-use activities, and links to space-related lesson plans.

www.spaceday.org/

THINKQUEST'S INTERNET CHALLENGE AND THINKQUEST JUNIOR

Students interested in collaborating with others around the world on topics such as their views on aging and older people, ways to become more knowledgeable about Shakespeare and his works, fractals and how they are made, and human nutritional needs have created over 4,500 Web sites for other students, available at the ThinkQuest Web site. Developed for students aged twelve through nineteen, ThinkQuest's Internet Challenge has brought together teams of two or three students from around the world to deepen and share their knowledge through the Internet. Winning entries from this year's ThinkQuest Junior, open to American students in grades 4–6, included Web sites focused on Greek mythology, U.S. civil rights, Hawaii's wetlands, and Peregrine falcons.

www.thinkquest.org/

RESEARCH SUPPORTS PROJECT-BASED LEARNING AND TECHNOLOGY

A growing body of academic research supports the use of project-based learning in schools as a way to engage students, cut absenteeism, boost cooperative learning skills, and improve student achievement. Those benefits are enhanced when technology is used to promote critical thinking and communication. Following are synopses of several studies on project-based learning:

Improved Student Engagement, Collaboration, and Achievement

In a five-year study, researchers at SRI International found that technology-using students in Challenge 2000 Multimedia Project classrooms outperformed non-technology-using students in communication skills, teamwork, and problem solving. The Center for Learning in Technology researchers, led by Bill Penuel, found increased student engagement, greater responsibility for learning, increased peer collaboration skills, and greater achievement gains by students who had been labeled as low-achievers. The project conducted a performance assessment designed to measure students' skills in constructing a presentation aimed at a particular audience.

Students from Multimedia Project classrooms outperformed comparison classrooms in all three areas scored by researchers and teachers: student content, attention to audience, and design. The Multimedia Project involves completing one to four interdisciplinary multimedia projects a year that integrate real-world issues and practices.

Source: SRI International Evaluation of Challenge 2000 Multimedia Project (2000). Center for Technology in Learning, http://pblmm.k12.ca.us/sri/SRIEvaluation.htm

Higher Mathematics Achievement in the Middle Grades

Educational Testing Service researcher Harold Wenglinsky analyzed data from the mathematics portion of the 1996 National Assessment of Educational Progress given to 6,227 fourth graders and 7,146 eighth graders. He found that a combination of project-based learning and technology resulted in achievement gains and that the effectiveness of computers in the classroom depended on how they were used. Wenglinsky concluded that computers used for drill and practice had a negative effect on student achievement. Computers used for real-world applications such as spreadsheets or to simulate relationships or changing variables were related to increases in student achievement.

Source: Does It Compute: The Relations Between Educational Technology and Student Achievement (1995). Princeton, N.J.: Policy Information Center, 1998. http://www.ets.org/research/pic/pir.html

Successful School Restructuring

A five-year study by University of Wisconsin-Madison researchers found that structural school reform works when "disciplined inquiry"—a key component of project-based learning—is incorporated in the reform. Other components leading to reform included engaging students in activities that build on prior knowledge and allow them to apply that knowledge to new situations, and connecting students' school activities to value beyond the confines of the school. The study analyzed data from more than fifteen hundred elementary, middle, and high schools between 1990 and 1995.

Source: Successful School Restructuring: A Report to the Public and Educators. Center on Organization and Restructuring of Schools. Madison, Wisc.: Board of Regents of the University of Wisconsin System, 1995. http://llanes.panam.edu/journal/library/Vol1No1/success.html

From Low-Performing to High-Achieving District

The Center for Children and Technology (CCT) at the Education Development Center monitored a two-year technology trial in the Union City School District in September 1993. The study found that after multimedia technology was used to support project-based learning, eighth graders in Union City scored 27 percentage points higher than students from other urban and special needs school districts on statewide tests in reading, math, and writing achievement. The study also found a decrease in absenteeism and an increase in student transfers into the school. Four years earlier, the state had been considering a takeover of district management due to Union City's failing forty of fifty-two indicators of school effectiveness. Today, the district is one of New Jersey's best.

Source: Union City Interactive Multimedia Education Trial (1996).
http://www.edc.org/CCT/ccthome/tech_rept/CCTR3

High Scores in High School Mathematics

A three-year study of two British secondary schools—one that used open-ended projects and one that used more traditional direct instruction—found striking differences in mathematics understanding and achievement. In the study, Jo Boaler—now associate professor of education at Stanford University—found that students at the project-based school did better than those at the more traditional school both on math problems requiring analytical or conceptual thought and on those requiring memorization of a rule or formula. Three times as many students at the project-based school received the top grade on the national examination in math.

Source: "Open and Closed Mathematics: Student Experiences and Understandings." *Journal for Research in Mathematics Education,* 1997, 29(1), 41–62.

See accompanying DVD for related video clip.

3

Laptops for Learning

ROBERTA FURGER

A sixth grader lowers a temperature probe inside a beaker full of hot water. Two classmates stare intently at a laptop computer screen, watching as a graph dynamically changes when a chip of melting ice gradually lowers the water temperature. Another student sits poised, pen in hand, ready to record every detail of the science lab on a procedure sheet.

"It's melting!" exclaims one student.

"The temperature is going down, all right," agrees another.

"When the ice is gone, we'll hit stop," directs the one who has been given the job of data collector for the group.

This popular science lab activity at the Mott Hall School is the culmination of several days' worth of exploration into the heat of fusion, or the

amount of heat required to melt a solid substance into its liquid form. Throughout the room, the sixth graders are working in groups of five, each team responsible for setting up its station, conducting the experiment, and then analyzing the results. Their tools consist of a mix of standard lab equipment (such as a beaker and a triple beam balance) and some decidedly high-tech additions, including a temperature probe connected to a laptop computer and software that records, graphs, and displays the changing water temperature in real time. In addition to temperature probes, other probes can gauge pressure and sound, providing students with access to a low-cost version of professional scientific instruments.

Sixth-grade science teacher Mercedes Diez had begun the class with a quick refresher on phase-change operations, but quickly turned the activity over to her students. They troubleshoot when one of the probes isn't working properly, consider possible causes for unexpected results, and brainstorm ways to present their findings to their classmates. For her part, Diez serves as a facilitator. She responds to the occasional question or poses one of her own, always encouraging her students to take their analysis *just a little bit further.*

HARLEM TECHNOLOGY PIONEERS

Mott Hall is a math, science, and technology academy in New York Community School District 6. The fourth-through-eighth-grade magnet school sits on the edge of the Harlem campus of the City College of New York. And it's one of a growing number of schools in the country where every student and every teacher has a laptop computer for personal use. A recent study by District 6 found that reading and mathematics achievement had risen by ten points for laptop-using students, who also had a higher attendance rate.

> Reading and mathematics achievement rose by ten points for laptop-using students.

Mott Hall opened in 1986, and for the first ten years of its existence the school offered a rigorous but fairly traditional approach to education. But everything started to change in 1996. That's when a class of fifth graders and their teacher became pioneers in the use of laptop computers in a K–12 school.

Mott Hall students use science probes and laptops for data collection.

"We saw the introduction of laptops as a wonderful opportunity to reexamine our curriculum *and* to confront the Digital Divide," says Principal Mirian Acosta-Sing. With the vast majority of students living in poverty, purchasing a home computer wasn't an option for Mott Hall families. But parents, Acosta-Sing recalls, "immediately understood what laptops could do for their kids—academically and in terms of job skills." Together, parents and staff developed policies to ensure the safety of students traveling to and from school, created a payment plan that relied on the contribution of families and the school district, and began troubleshooting everything from curriculum delivery to basic repair and maintenance.

Over the next five years, Acosta-Sing and her staff built on that first pilot project, slowly adding classes and grade levels to the growing contingent of laptop pioneers. Finally, in the fall of 1999, the last class received their laptops.

A FOCUS ON PROJECT-BASED LEARNING

Visitors to Mott Hall don't have to look hard for evidence of how laptop computers have changed teaching and learning. While sixth graders are conducting experiments with temperature probes, fifth graders are creating scale models of kites in Excel spreadsheets and reading poems about Harlem, inspired by digital photographs taken by students at nearby St. Nicholas Park. Seventh graders are creating business plans as part of a project on entrepreneurship. And the eighth graders, who will soon be graduating and moving on to some of the city's most prestigious high schools, are creating a digital photo album and conducting scientific research on methane gas emissions, coral reef bleaching, and dozens of other topics of their own choosing.

Every classroom and every hallway is a showcase for student work. Artwork, essays, poems, and science posters cover the walls. And everywhere, there are laptop computers. In one classroom, students are logging on to an Internet chess site to play against a far-away opponent. In another, a group of students are putting the final touches on a multimedia presentation. Students manipulate temperature probes and swap network cards as easily as they might replace the lead in a mechanical pencil or verify a computation on a calculator.

Students swap network cards as easily as they might replace the lead in a mechanical pencil.

Teachers, too, have come a long way, thanks in large part to the school's built-from-the-ground-up approach to professional development. From its first day as a laptop pilot school, Mott Hall has relied on the expertise of its most experienced teachers to advance the technical and curriculum savvy of its entire staff. Staff development days are used to showcase exemplary teaching units. More experienced teachers mentor their colleagues, opening up their classrooms for observation and taking the time after a long school day to meet and plan lessons. Partnerships with local universities, businesses, and other organizations provide yet another level of support and training for Mott Hall staff.

Through one innovative partnership with City College of New York, fourteen Mott Hall students work in seven different science and engineering labs. For example, two eighth-grade girls were mentored by a biology graduate student in conducting research on the effect of light on microorganisms in coral reef ecosystems. The lab was interested in the relationship between the ozone layer and destruction of coral reefs. As one of the girls said during an interview at the lab, "I think it's a privilege to be here. I found it to be really fun and it expanded my horizons. Now I can see I have more choices for jobs."

Laptops aid students in kite design.

GO FLY A KITE

A steady rain is falling outside Room 502, where Sandra Skea's class of fifth graders are putting the finishing touches on a second generation of handmade kites. At one table, Brandon is attaching a new tail to his kite in hopes of helping it fly longer and higher. At another, Lisbeth and Vanessa are working intently on their tetrahedron kite, a three-tier design made out of multicolored tissue paper and straws and held together with lots and lots of glue. Throughout the room, tables are covered with the stuff homemade kites are made of—paper, straws, tinfoil, skewers, string—all contributed by students, their teacher, family members, and friends.

Already students have spent several days on the interdisciplinary unit. They've written poetry and prose, studied such diverse topics as electromagnetism and the use of kite flying in celebrations, and developed a keen understanding of principles of ratios and proportions as they designed and refined their kites—on the computer and then by hand.

Having been somewhat less than successful in their first kite-flying expedition, Skea and her students are now back at the drawing board, refining their original designs. As soon as the rain stops, they'll put their second round of creations to the test.

But the point of the project isn't to see whose kite flies the highest or stays in the air the longest—and that's not how the veteran teacher will be grading her students. Instead, Skea explains, the rubrics, or criteria, by which she'll be grading students address how well they work together, the amount and quality of their research, the thoroughness of their writing, and how well they planned their first—and then refined their second—kite design.

"The kite falling on the ground is not going to cause them to fail," Skea adds matter-of-factly. "The purpose was that they thought to try a new design and that they're starting to connect purpose to design. That's the science part of it, that's what's behind the lesson."

Digital photographs taken by students inspire poetry writing at Mott Hall.

NEW CHALLENGES, NEW OPPORTUNITIES

If imitation is the sincerest form of flattery, then the staff and students at Mott Hall should feel truly honored. In September 2001 a new school—Mott Hall II—opened in New York City, building on the philosophy and methods developed at the original Mott Hall. In fact, all the schools in New York Community School District 6 are now adopting the laptop model. And throughout the country, hundreds of public schools are embracing the use of laptops to support student learning and teacher development.

For their part, Acosta-Sing and her staff are moving ahead to experiment with new technology tools. With the help of a pilot grant, they and their students are investigating ways in which handheld computers can support project-based learning. "We don't have a script," says Acosta-Sing. "We're just kind of learning as we go."

THE POSITIVE EFFECTS OF "LAPTOP LEARNING" ON STUDENT ACHIEVEMENT AND TEACHER INSTRUCTION

The portability and convenience of laptop computers is leading to improved student learning and teaching styles. A three-year study of the use of laptop computers in schools has found positive effects on student writing and collaboration, and deeper involvement with schoolwork. Teachers also benefited, changing their teaching style from an emphasis on lecturing to fostering more independent student learning. They also reported greater confidence in the use of technology.

The study was conducted after three years of implementation of Microsoft's Anytime Anywhere Learning program by Rockman et al, a San Francisco-based independent research firm. The program began in the fall of 1996 with fifty-two schools in the United States and has expanded to more than eight hundred schools with 125,000 students and teachers, including Mott Hall School. The study used questionnaires, completed logs, and surveys to gather data from more than five hundred students and teachers who use laptops, who were matched and compared with groups of students and teachers who were not laptop users.

Improved Writing, Student Collaboration, and Active Teaching

- Access to technology improves students' writing and encourages collaboration among students. Laptop computers supported all elements of the writing process from research to drafting to presentation. Students worked in groups more often and at their own pace, using their laptops to learn how to process and organize assignments, as well as how to work with others. Ninety percent of teachers who used laptops assigned projects in which students taught other students, compared with 46 percent of teachers who did not use laptops.

- Students who use laptops are more involved in their schoolwork. More laptop students explored topics on their own (80 percent of laptop students versus 46 percent of non-laptop students), revised their work more often, and worked on longer-term projects (80 percent compared to 38 percent of non-laptop students).

- Teachers who use laptops use a more constructivist approach to teaching. Constructivist teaching is based on research showing that learning is deeper and more meaningful when students are actively involved in the learning process rather than passively receiving information. Teachers who use laptops lectured less often than before—once a week on average. Ninety percent of those educators stated that students in their classes teach each other, rather than relying solely on the teacher for direction, and 83 percent said they learn from their students.

- Teachers who use laptops feel more empowered in their classrooms. Teachers who use laptops have a greater sense of control over their responsibilities for instruction and managing student learning. They also have greater confidence in using technology tools in eight measurable categories, such as word processing, e-mail, and the Internet, than their peers who do not use laptops.

"Laptop learning" is spreading around the world, with more than 1,250 such schools in the United Kingdom, Belgium, and Canada.

Source: www.microsoft.com/education/aal.mspx

Handhelds Go to Class

The same low-cost devices used by business professionals to keep their calendars and contact numbers—and even to send e-mail and surf the Internet—have found their way into classrooms as important learning tools. Handheld computers, those notecard-sized devices also known as personal digital assistants (PDAs), are appealing to a growing number of administrators, teachers, and students for their portability, affordability, and increasing versatility.

"The economic factor is a really important piece of the puzzle," says Darrell Walery, district director of technology for Consolidated District 230 in the Chicago suburb of Orland Park. "I can't buy a laptop for every kid, but I may be able to buy a handheld for every kid," especially when the price gets down to $100—"which I think is going to happen pretty soon."

> I can't buy a laptop for every kid, but I may be able to buy a handheld.

In one of the largest school implementations to date, District 230 equipped its three high schools with 2,200 Palm IIIxe's in the fall of 2000. Interested teachers were given classroom sets or students could buy or lease the miniature computers.

31

AN EARLY CONVERT

Laurie Ritchey, a biology teacher at Carl Sandburg High School, was one "early adopter" who quickly incorporated handhelds in her classes. Besides the speed, portability, and ease of reducing complicated tasks to the push of a button, she says, "what you rope is kids' enthusiasm."

Ritchey experienced their enthusiasm in an assignment to create an "ecological footprint," a measurement of the human impact on nature in terms of the land and water used to produce the resources humans consume and to take in all the waste humans make.

Handheld computers with attachable keyboards aid collection and sharing of data.

The assignment started with Ritchey "beaming" worksheet questions—transferring information between two handhelds via an infrared ray. Each student then "beamed" the questions to another student, and so on, through the class roll, "as opposed to handing out paper." The students' job was to record information on the handhelds such as how much they ate, how much energy they used, how much their laundry weighed, how much garbage they generated, and the square footage of their homes. The students were able to bring their PDAs home to collect data from their home environment.

Once the data were collected, the students returned to school and logged on to the Ecological Footprint Web site. They input the information into the school computer through the method of communicating with a desktop computer called "synchronization" or "hot sync." The Web site then translated the student data into number of hectares of land needed to support themselves and their families.

THE OUTDOOR LABORATORY

For another assignment, the students attached a probe, a special sensing device, to the PDAs and took them outside to measure oxygen concentrations in a pond. Probes were dropped into various areas and depths of the water to measure the effect of sunlight on plant growth. That information was instantly graphed, using special software. Students were able to test a variable and instantly see a live, moving graph illustrating their results in real time as opposed to the traditional method of obtaining data and graphing it hours later. "The instantaneous generation of information," says Ritchey, "leads to more accurate conclusions during the lab process."

Use of the handhelds has not been confined to science classes. English teacher Jean Lombaer used the handhelds with a class of sophomores reading below grade level and witnessed noticeable improvements in their work. Her students used a flashcard program to enter vocabulary words and definitions and track right and wrong answers.

"I'm not going to tell you that it's because the Palm is better than flashcards, but it's brand new for kids, and the delight of working with new technology caused them to learn a lot of the things I wanted them to learn," she says. As another aid to memorizing vocabulary, her students used software to draw a picture to accompany the words.

The handhelds encourage greater peer editing, Lombaer adds, noting that students can easily transfer draft copies of papers to each other and make revisions using inexpensive keyboards. Her students are more willing to revise when they can type in words rather

> The delight of working with new technology caused [the kids] to learn a lot of the things I wanted them to learn.

than having to write by hand. If tapping in letters with a stylus were the only option, she says, the tiny computers would be not be nearly as useful. She also used the PDAs for tests, revamping the format so that beaming of answers among students was an asset rather than an automatic "F" grade. She arranged students in small groups and required that their answers involve group consultation.

CONNECTING TO WALL STREET

During a study of the Great Depression, Stagg High School social studies teacher Josh Barron used an Internet program to call up current stock tables and give students an idea of market fluctuations. Given "$5,000" to buy and sell, students beamed their results to Barron, whose class comparison of students who gained and lost was immediately put into graph form. The students also wrote reports on the PDAs using the supplementary keyboards.

A visit to a pond with PDAs and probes helps make science study real for Stagg students.

Kim Onak, a Stagg biology teacher who keeps a set of handhelds for her special education class, says the assignment and project planner capabilities of the handhelds—their original functions—should not be underestimated. Her students are much more organized with the PDAs and use them to keep track of grades. They also use them to input measurements in the English system and convert them to millimeters and to draw cells that become animated to depict cell division in action.

Ritchey, the Sandburg High biology teacher, notes that uses continue to multiply, proving that handhelds are not just the latest techno-fad. "We're definitely on an evolutionary trail," Ritchey says. "It's going to get better and better."

See accompanying DVD for related video clip.

More Fun Than a Barrel of … Worms?!

DIANE CURTIS

Curiosity about a classmate's cystic fibrosis leads to an investigation of genetics. Desire to produce a school yearbook veers into a study of refraction and other properties of light. Discovery that the World Wrestling Federation is listed on the New York Stock Exchange turns into creation of a business newspaper and an in-depth look at the Great Depression.

At Newsome Park Elementary School in Newport News, Virginia, where projects dominate classroom work, learning takes twists and turns rarely possible in a more traditional, fixed-curriculum setting.

"They're engaged. They want to be here," says Principal Peter Bender. During recess and lunch, he routinely overhears students sharing information about their projects and brainstorming about how to make them better. "In thirty years, I don't think I've ever heard kids talk like that." And test scores have risen across the board at this school, which has about 40 percent white, 50 percent black, and nearly 60 percent low-income students. Between 1997 and 2000, the percentage of fifth graders passing the Virginia Standards of Learning test increased from 35 percent to 65 percent in math, 52 percent to 79 percent in science, and 53 percent to 65 percent in English. African American students also narrowed the gap between their scores and those of white students.

They're engaged. They want to be here.

MORE ENTHUSIASTIC LEARNERS

Bender and his staff have worked hard to create a program that meets students' academic, emotional, and creative needs. The recipe for success includes morning meetings, looping (in which teachers stay with one class for two years), community service, teacher professional development, and state-of-the-art technology. Parents report that the "What-did-you-do-at-school-today?" question no longer gets just a grunt or a one-word non-answer. Instead, dinner table conversations are nonstop discussions about projects—from night skies and modes of transportation to house construction and hostile takeovers. "There's actually a visible hunger to learn," says Ingo Schiller, a parent of two Newsome Park students.

THE PROJECTS

In Robert Lirange's fourth-grade class, students count out $40 raised from selling plants from their "Flower Power" business. When their interest in the stock market was piqued by the World Wrestling Federation's listing on the New York Stock Exchange, they decided to focus one of their twice-a-year projects on the stock market. The nine- and ten-year-olds learned how to read stock tables, researched and tracked the

progress of companies in which they "invested," and studied the Great Depression, the history of the market, and its effect on the economy. They produced a business section of a newspaper and distributed it throughout the school. When the concepts of net and gross profits were firmly entrenched and when buying and selling became a little "stale," as Lirange puts it, the students decided to create a plant business and sell shares in the business. "They're doing real-life things, doing it for a purpose," says Lirange. "Kids are just so much more enthusiastic when I have them applying their own knowledge."

WHAT HAPPENS AT NIGHT

Kindergartners from Nancy Mason's class are lining up for a "field trip with a purpose" to the Virginia Living Museum. The outing is part of the class project, "While You Were Sleeping . . . A Project About Night!" Mason and other adult chaperones are armed with clipboards to document the students' findings about nocturnal animals and their habitats. The "While You Were Sleeping" project has included a trip to a planetarium, listening to such stories as "Moonflower" and "Nightmare in My Closet," investigating why spiders spin their webs at night and observing phases of the moon over a three-week period. They also interviewed fourth graders who were doing a project on bats. "I learn more than the kids do," says Mason.

CONCERN FOR A CLASSMATE

Teacher Billie Hetrick's second graders are compiling information about cystic fibrosis, which they adopted as a project out of concern for a classmate's frequent trips to the hospital and school nurse's office. "Why does she have to take medicine so often?" "What is cystic fibrosis and how is it caused?" "Is there a cure?" they asked. The children studied the disease on the Internet, peppered two representatives from the Cystic Fibrosis

Foundation with questions, and raised over $1,200 for cystic fibrosis research through a Cystic Fibrosis Math Challenge and walkathon.

REAL-WORLD APPLICATIONS

Math, writing, reading, and other subjects are interwoven into classroom projects and applied as in the real world. Use of spreadsheets, PowerPoint presentations, computer slide shows, drawing and word processing programs, and digital cameras and scanners become second nature to the students. Careful planning ensures that they meet state academic standards. Lirange's fourth graders, for example, fulfilled twenty-four state standards during the stock market project, including estimating and measuring weight and mass, writing effective narratives and explanations, using evidence to support opinions in oral communication, investigating and understanding the interaction of plants in an ecosystem, and communicating through application software. When he couldn't fit some of the standards, such as studying the Civil War, into the project, he taught them separately.

Fourth graders fulfilled twenty-four state standards during one project.

"We've got to know our curriculum. We've got to know the standards inside and out," says Patty Vreeland, a kindergarten and first-grade teacher, who adds that teachers must be willing to work harder to ensure that projects are meaningful learning experiences. "Even though it looks like the kids are doing all the hard work, there's a lot of planning that goes on behind it to make sure that the work is there for them," Vreeland explains. Newsome Park teachers use a structure created by University of Alberta Professor Sylvia Chard, coauthor of *The Project Approach.* Phase 1 involves engaging children in an initial discussion of a topic. Phase 2 involves field work, meeting with experts, gathering information from the Internet, and compiling the information into multimedia portfolios.

Phase 3 concludes with a presentation of the project work. At Newsome Park, that means inviting parents, community members, and staff and students from other schools to "Project Day."

POISED PRESENTATIONS

During a regular school day, students in Cathy Huemer's first-grade class demonstrate the poise and knowledge that wins them accolades from visitors on Project Day. The class is finishing up its project on worms, and a pigtailed girl digs through a bin of sand, soil, leaves, and paper strips to show off one of the wiggly creatures. "If it's a grownup, it has a clitellum," she says, gliding smoothly over a word that would give adults pause and pointing to a thick, pinkish band on the worm. Asked how a worm breathes, she doesn't miss a beat. "It breathes through its skin," she replies.

> Teachers must be willing to work harder to ensure that projects are meaningful learning experiences.

Students themselves sing the praises of project work and express its impact on their learning. "You can find out more than by just reading about it in a book," one child says. "It's more fun because you don't just sit there and take notes all day—in one ear, out the other," says another. "If you find it yourself, it stays in your brain," sums up a third student.

Principal Bender and the teachers concur, adding that discipline problems and absenteeism are reduced, while children learn to count on each other for feedback and see that their efforts do make a difference—from contributing to disease research to organizing blood drives to creating antipollution brochures. Bender says projects make it easier to evaluate his teachers because "the children's products are so public, their presentations so compelling." It can be more difficult to persuade some teachers of a style of teaching and learning so foreign to their own school experiences. "The old saying that teachers teach the way they were taught is very true," Bender points out. But resistance to projects doesn't last long once teachers seen the enthusiasm, excitement, and quality of student work. "The children actually sell it," Bender reports. "It's harder to teach this way, but a hundred times more rewarding."

It's harder to teach

this way, but a

hundred times

more rewarding.

Bugscope

Magnifying the Connections Between Students, Science, and Scientists

MILTON CHEN

What if expensive but important scientific instruments such as the Hubble telescope, electron microscopes, or even remote sensing satellites were on the network, and students could queue up requests for their use? This is not a farfetched scenario.

—Dr. Elliot Soloway, professor of computer science and education, University of Michigan, 1994

In 1996, in a story filmed by The George Lucas Educational Foundation for its *Learn & Live* documentary, Jim Dieckmann's fourth- and fifth-grade students in Chula Vista, California, studied insects for an in-depth project. They collected specimens, obtained information from Web sites on entomology, and created multimedia reports. Together with their teacher, the students developed a set of guidelines known as an *assessment rubric* to evaluate their reports according to use of text, images, graphics, and sound.

A special school-university partnership provided these students with even more powerful learning experiences. Students sent their insects to nearby San Diego State University, which was connected to their school via fiber-optic cable. Through two-way audio and video, scientists Steve Barlow and Kathy Williams guided the students in examining their insect specimens under an electron microscope. The students were visibly excited as they prepared for each online session with the scientists. Many fourth graders have never heard of an electron microscope, but these ten- and eleven-year-olds were actually using one. A related multimedia feature (digital video clips) shows how this project unfolds.

Many fourth graders have never heard of an electron microscope, but these ten- and eleven-year-olds were actually using one.

GOVERNMENT AND BUSINESS PARTNERSHIP PROVIDES ACCESS TO ADVANCED TECHNOLOGY

Five years ago, that project's use of advanced technology might have seemed out of reach for most schools. However, in 1999, another innovative partnership with the scientific community made the project done by Jim Dieckmann's class available to potentially every school in the country with an Internet connection.

With funding from the National Science Foundation, Illinois Consolidated Telephone Company, and others, the University of Illinois's Beckman Institute for Advanced Science and Technology launched Bugscope, where students around the country capture insect specimens, send them to the university, and then, through the Internet, control the university's $600,000 environmental scanning electron microscope (ESEM) for a two-hour period to view their insects. With the encouragement of funders in business and government, this partnership is one of a growing number making remote operation of sophisticated scientific instruments available to K–12 schools.

Beckman scientists designed Bugscope as a Web-based project to be low-cost and sustainable by a small research group. They designed a Web interface for a remote control panel so that students, using their classroom computer and a Web browser, can control the microscope as they discuss their insects with the university's entomologists. Bugscope also helps to close the Digital Divide—classrooms with minimal equipment, whether in the inner city or an isolated rural area, can still take advantage of Bugscope. Some schools have accessed Bugscope using a single computer and modem. Others have sophisticated computer labs with high-speed Internet connections. The project is available to K–12 schools at no cost.

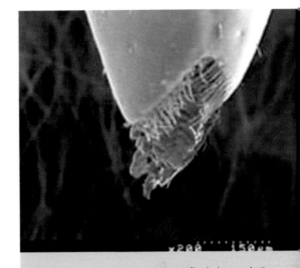

Sand bee mouthparts magnified through San Diego State University's electron microscope.

CHANNELING ENTHUSIASM FOR BUGS

Since the first classroom logged on to Bugscope in March 1999, more than fifteen hundred students in almost sixty schools have participated, from kindergarten through high school. In 1999 alone, students collected over four thousand images from the electron microscope. Bugscope's goal is to reach up to a hundred classrooms a year. Dr. Clint Potter, project codirector, believes that "for most youngsters, bugs are second in popularity only to dinosaurs. We are hoping to channel that enthusiasm for bugs to get students interested in and excited about scientific research."

At a school in the Ozarks, a tenth-grade biology class used the electron microscope to examine small aquatic insects as indicators of water quality. The region faces issues of water pollution caused by runoff from chicken, hog, and cattle operations. The high school students collected insect larvae, daphnia, and snail eggs from local water sources and examined them under the microscope, making a total of 230 images.

DOING "REAL SCIENCE"

Teachers submitting evaluations emphasize the students' excitement and motivation and comment on the project's effective use of the Internet. As Pam Van Walleghen, a teacher at Urbana Middle School in Urbana, Illinois, testified, "Giving students the opportunity to do `real science' using state-of-the-art technology is about as exciting as education can get." Bugscope engages students in the scientific process and gives them experience with the realities of scientific research.

This is about as exciting as education can get.

Bugscope grew out of Chickscope, another Beckman Institute project that allowed students to study magnetic resonance images (MRI) of developing chicken embryos via the Web. Chickscope encountered problems with the high cost of the technology and the time commitment required from professional scientists. It now continues as an image database.

HIGH SCHOOL AND COLLEGE STUDENTS ACT AS PROJECT STAFF

One key to the sustainability of Bugscope is the training of local high school students, who prepare the specimens and perform the initial microscope setup. Given the high cost of professional staff, a University of Illinois entomology major is employed to participate in the online discussion with students. Teachers report that their students respond very

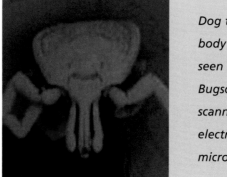

Dog tick, full body view, as seen through Bugscope's scanning electron microscope.

positively to communicating with the Bugscope team in real time while they are controlling the microscope.

The Bugscope project has also automated many project administration and data handling tasks. Online applications from teachers are automatically archived into a database for review and scheduling by staff. During each online session, images are stored for later retrieval by the classrooms or other interested groups.

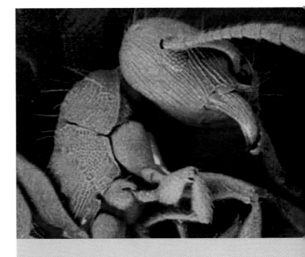

Image of an ant, via Bugscope.

This developing movement to place high-powered scientific instrumentation in the hands of students continues. Other remote-access projects involve students in using the Goldstone Apple Valley Radio Telescope and in exploring simulated Martian terrain using a Lego micro-rover.

In just seven years, Professor Elliot Soloway's vision of the Internet has become a reality, connecting students and teachers to scientists and their own high-tech tools.

Related Web site: bugscope.beckman.uiuc.edu

7

Assistive Technology Enhances Learning for All

LISA WAHL

- A kindergarten student with cerebral palsy, who can't speak and has limited movement, uses a talking switch to act as the "caller" for a game of Red Light/Green Light. A light touch to the switch announces "green light" and sends her classmates running. A second touch causes the device to say "red light" when she wants her classmates to stop.

- A student who can comprehend history at the ninth-grade level but can read only at the third-grade level gains access to his history textbook with the help of a computer that scans and reads text out loud. The computer displays the material as it reads, so the student can understand the graphic features of the textbook, including timelines and graphs.

Much of this article was developed for the Alliance for Technology Access, in collaboration with the WestEd Regional Technology in Education Consortium's Learning for Everyone initiative. These and related materials can be found at http://www.ataccess.org/resources/atk12.

- A child with extreme dyslexia uses an AlphaSmart laptop word processor—a small, rugged keyboarding device—to take notes that are later transferred to a computer for editing.

- A child who can't listen and take notes simultaneously gets copies of notes from other students, who have used carbonless copy paper so he can focus his attention on listening during the lesson.

- A one-handed typist uses a standard keyboard in which the key locations have been rearranged (using a free software utility and some labels) to optimize the position of the most frequently typed keys. Such a typist could also use one of the keyboards specially designed for just five fingers, with as few as eight keys.

WE ALL HAVE SPECIAL NEEDS: ASSISTIVE TECHNOLOGY FOR EACH LEARNING STYLE

Education for students with disabilities now takes place in a wide range of settings, from full inclusion in mainstream classes to special day classes that allow intensive support for particular skills. It is a time when expectations are higher for *every* child. Those expectations and educational options are often made possible by assistive technology (AT) devices that make it easier for all students to participate in classroom activities.

Now, expectations are higher for *every* child.

While AT includes a set of federally mandated services and equipment for students with disabilities, the term also refers to valuable tools and strategies for including students with a wide range of learning styles in classroom activities. AT can be a triangular pencil grip, a talking calculator, a larger computer monitor, or a voice amplifier for a teacher with vocal cord strain. All these examples reflect the individual nature of assessing when and how a device will make teaching and learning more effective—as well as the benefits of many kinds of assistive technologies to people without disabilities.

The 1997 federal reauthorization of the Individuals with Disabilities Education Act (IDEA) states that school districts must provide assistive technology to eligible children if needed to ensure the provision of a free appropriate public education. Educators across the country are struggling to consider each student's need for assistive technology. Along with the time it takes to assess each child's needs, other barriers to implementing AT include a lack of AT-experienced teachers and related personnel, few sources of staff training focusing on education, and need for additional funding. As with any educational technology, the challenge is to integrate AT as a tool to provide access to the standard curriculum. Even with these barriers, examples of successful uses abound.

Large keyboard icons aid students with physical and/or visual impairments.

SUCCESS STORIES IN ACTION

It's reading time in a second-grade classroom in Contra Costa County in the San Francisco Bay Area. About half the children select a book from the classroom library and return to their desks. One child uses a transparent yellow film overlay on each page to increase the contrast in the print. Another uses a black card with a long horizontal window cut out that allows him to see just a single line at a time. A third child with reading difficulties moves to the computer and puts on headphones. He selects the text file for a book that has been scanned into the computer. The computer can read every word aloud but the teacher chooses a different option, which allows the student to click on difficult words and hear them pronounced. The teacher also sets the print size and font to one that she knows is optimal for this child's vision.

In Fremont Unified School District in nearby Alameda County, one of fourteen disabled students—two with poor vision, four in electric wheelchairs that they are able to maneuver by themselves, three who are not able to speak due to physical or neurological disabilities, and several with developmental disabilities—leads the class in the Pledge of Allegiance. The words are programmed into the youngster's Deltatalker, a device that speaks in response to commands sent by a head-mounted infrared pointer. Another student uses her Deltatalker by pressing a single finger to one key to say hello. The teacher uses both spoken words and sign language. When she writes on the chalkboard, an aide writes the same thing on a smaller chalkboard less than three feet away from a student with poor vision.

MathPad software enhances student abilities to practice computation.

STUDENTS HELPING STUDENTS

A "volunteers welcome" sign hangs on the door at various times in the day. This sign invites older students who have been licensed through a training program on disability awareness, safety, and volunteering to come in and assist with a recreational or study period. Volunteers are particularly helpful in setting up and putting away materials and in giving one-to-one assistance in reading, writing, and other class work.

Throughout the room, computer stations on height-adjustable carts provide adapted keyboards that include a large flat surface along with adjustable "key" size, as well as trackballs, which are easier to use than a mouse for some users with motor difficulties. During math, an adapted keyboard can be used with a number keypad overlay. With software called MathPad, students who can't hold a pencil or who have fine motor problems find it much easier to solve problems on the computer because the digits are clear and properly aligned. The software tells them if they answered correctly or not. The software also allows numbers to be spoken as they are entered and also allows the teacher to prepare a customized problem list for each student.

SLANT BOARDS, VELCRO STRIPS, AND PARENT BINDERS

Math Bingo is another classroom activity that is under way. Slant boards (boards propped up on angled book stands) are used to support the bingo cards at the best visual angle for each student. As each number is pulled, it is shown, and the teacher or a volunteer says it out loud. In a simple adaptation to make playtime more enjoyable for some disabled students, paper dolls sport Velcro strips for easier dressing.

When students leave for the day, they may take a binder with them that provides parents with information about progress toward specific goals and objectives, as well as any homework assignments. This is particularly important when technology tools (such as communication devices) travel between school and home. Parent-teacher communication can facilitate consistency and effectiveness of use, a critically important connection for the learning of all our students.

8

Looping

The Best Kind of Déjà Vu

CYNTHIA ROBERTS

On the first day of school in rural Bucks County, Pennsylvania, Rachael Tubiello looked out into the eager faces of her tiny second graders and this is what she saw: old friends.

Tubiello's students are the same children she guided through the highs and lows of first grade. Together, students and teacher have advanced to the second grade through an innovative approach to learning known as *looping*.

Also called "continuous learning," "multiyear placement," or "family-style learning," looping—in which the same teacher remains with a group of students for two or more years—is a concept as old as the one-room schoolhouse. Yet its proponents say the practice has a solid place in the twenty-first-century classroom because it strengthens student-teacher bonds, improves test scores, expands time for instruction, increases parent participation, and reduces behavioral problems and placements in special education programs.

When Principal Janet Link approached Tubiello and asked whether she'd consider looping with her first graders, "I jumped on it because I loved my class that year," Tubiello recalls. "The end of first grade is such an amazing time. You want to keep going because it's just beginning to click." When a teacher has an opportunity to work with the same children for another year, she says, "you can take them to the next level of anything."

> **We don't change dentists every thirty-six weeks. It makes no sense to change teachers.**

Looping at Durham Nockamixon Elementary School began, as it does at many schools, when one teacher learned about the practice and found another willing to work as a team. (As one teacher moves up a grade, another must drop down to take the next group of children.)

"We don't change dentists every thirty-six weeks. Or pediatricians. Or auto mechanics," says educator Jim Grant, a passionate advocate of continuous learning and author of *The Looping Handbook.* "It makes no sense to change teachers."

GOOD FOR STUDENTS, TEACHERS, AND THE BUDGET

Although staff must prepare to teach at least two grade levels, looping costs a district virtually nothing. Since it requires extra classroom preparation, it usually attracts a school's most energetic teachers and gives them an opportunity to push the limits of their professional development, Grant finds. "The very best staff development experience a teacher can have is to change grade levels" and experience the class at a new developmental stage. "A seven-year-old isn't a large version of a six-year-old."

Linda McBride teaches a multigrade looped class. Each September she welcomes a new group of first graders while the other half of her class consists of her second graders from the previous year. "I really like it," she grins. "I like having the kids come back to me. The little first grader who's not even reading in the beginning of the year . . . you get such a sense of accomplishment when you grow with them."

Because looping teachers already know their students' strengths, and the children understand what's required of them, September isn't lost to establishing classroom routines or student assessment. Advocates like to say the first day of school is actually the 181st day of school for a child in a looping classroom. "There's no lost time," McBride says. "You can just pull out the books and get started."

Principal Link says her school sees "stronger readers going into third grade" and few special education placements, trends reported by other districts that have adopted looping. In a looping classroom, Link says, "teachers feel they can give kids extra time to grow because they know they'll be with them (the following year)." Looping allows for a wait-and-see approach to a student who's struggling. Otherwise, a teacher may feel pressured to move a student whose grasp of material is tentative into special education classes for fear of not responding to the child's needs.

The Attleboro, Massachusetts, school district uses looping for all first- through eighth-grade students and has quantified its benefits. According to the district's surveys, retention rates—holding students back—in grades two through eight decreased by over 43 percent. Special education referrals dropped by more than 55 percent, and discipline and suspensions—especially in the middle schools—declined significantly while attendance rates improved for both students and teachers.

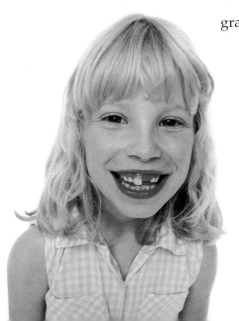

LOOPING'S PROS AND CONS

The downsides to looping are few but not insignificant. Parents worry about the prospect of a child drawing a weak teacher two years in a row. Teachers worry about being stuck with a difficult class. But for many parents, students, and teachers, the benefits far outweigh the deficits. "For young children, looping is ideal," Tubiello says. "They bond with you. They're more willing to take risks because they know you. They are willing to try something and make a mistake."

When students return to a teacher they already know, they naturally feel secure.

Come September, when students return to a teacher they already know, they naturally feel secure. Happily, the feeling is mutual. "With loopers in the second year, there are no first-day jitters," Tubiello says. "And I sleep like a baby the night before my second year begins. There's no stress worrying about whether they'll like me, too."

A Dozen Promising
Practices That Work

DIANE CURTIS, ROBERTA FURGER, AND MILTON CHEN

Despite numerous efforts to improve what happens in classrooms, many schools continue to follow decades-old models and roles. The traditional classroom has been a closed box, sealed off from access to people, ideas, and experiences beyond its walls. All knowledge was contained in the teacher's head and in the textbooks and other materials inside the classroom. Students sat at desks arranged in rows and worked individually. Roles were confined to a strict hierarchy—the teacher's job was to teach by talking; the student's job was to learn by memorizing.

As many have noted, the twenty-first century requires very different kinds of classrooms, bearing little resemblance to their ancestors. This chapter presents twelve tips from leading teachers and exemplary schools around the country that can break down the isolation of the classroom, open up its four walls, and breathe new life into teaching and learning. Many of these innovations introduce new roles for students and teachers and address how time is used during the school day. They all lead to closer relationships between students and teachers and among students themselves. Perhaps surprisingly, many of these practices do not require much in additional funds, if any, but only the willingness to "think outside the box."

1. PEER INSTRUCTION

Two or three times a week, the students in Kristy Beauvais's honors and Advanced Placement physics classes at Concord-Carlisle High School in Massachusetts teach each other. Using a method called "peer instruction" designed by Harvard professor Eric Mazur, Beauvais poses carefully constructed questions to her class before she begins to teach the topic. She then tallies the student answers and asks them to try to convince their class neighbors that theirs is the correct answer. "More often than not," Beauvais says, "the kids who are right are able to convince the other kids."

Besides the fact that the students are learning from peers who are "closer to their level of knowledge," she has witnessed a number of benefits with the method, including many documented by Mazur in his own research. Rather than tuning out long lectures, the students become involved. "The kids love it," Beauvais says. "It gets them talking, discussing. They're much more interested than if you just write something up on the board, and they remember it more than if you just tell them."

Beauvais's experience backs up Mazur's research on his own introductory physics classes at Harvard and the experiences of other college instructors. Mazur found that because students are forced to think through the arguments being developed, they make significant gains in conceptual understanding and problem solving. They can also assess their own understanding of a topic while in the classroom rather than try to puzzle out a complicated concept by themselves or, worse, learn that they don't understand a topic until it's too late—on the test.

2. CROSS-AGE TUTORING

Four days a week, sixteen seventh and eighth graders from Kazen Middle School in San Antonio, Texas, walk to a nearby elementary school to tutor younger children. The middle schoolers, chosen for the Coca-Cola Valued Youth Program for being at risk of dropping out of school, are paid $5.15 an hour for their labors, but the remuneration amounts to much more than dollars. Teacher Cathy Meyer, coordinator of the program at Kazen, says she has seen remarkable transformations of youngsters—from shy to confident, from uninterested in school to eager to do well, from gang members to respected school leaders. The act of teaching others is empowering, since the best way to learn something is to teach it. The younger students also look up to their older tutors and are eager for their leadership. The Intercultural Development Research Association, which created the program, reports that 98 percent of students in the program stay in school.

3. BRINGING LOCAL EXPERTS INTO THE CLASSROOM

Throughout New York state, members of the Performance Standards Consortium rely on experts from the business and academic world to evaluate student work and to bridge the gap between school and the larger community. At Urban Academy, a small alternative high school in New York City, outside experts—from attorneys and actors to historians and business managers—play a critical role in classroom learning and assessment.

Students present their culminating project work (part of a performance system of assessment) to a panel that includes experts in the relevant subject. "Outside experts ask questions that teachers might not pose," explains Urban Academy codirector and teacher Ann Cook, "and open up the educational activity or enterprise to the world." In addition to having local experts work with students in classes and on long-term projects, the school invites a member of the New York community to come and speak with students once a month. At these gatherings, called "conversations," the visitors talk about themselves and answer questions from students and staff. Says Cook, "It's a way of helping students to be more exposed to people with [a variety] of life experiences."

4. MULTI-AGE CLASSROOMS

It may be more work to make sure all topics are covered and each student is learning at an appropriate pace, but teacher Deborah Goodman is sold on grouping students from different grades in one class. In her class of eight kindergartners, five first graders, and five second graders at White Oak Elementary School in Edenton, North Carolina, students learn from each other, look out for each other, and help each other. The younger kids tend to catch on more quickly, and the older kids cement their knowledge by teaching others and becoming leaders—an opportunity less available in a more competitive single-grade class. Because she has the same children for three years, Goodman can look at the curriculum over a three-year span and move the kids as quickly as they are able to master the curriculum. Research on multi-age classrooms has pointed to such advantages as allowing for differences in learning styles and pace, giving older children leadership experience, and creating an environment with less competition and more cooperation and nurturing among students.

5. COOPERATIVE LEARNING

What cooperative learning is *not*, says English teacher Pam Hankins, is group grades, with the inevitable loss of individual responsibility that group grading entails. With group grades, she says, one or two kids always do most of the work and the slackers reap the benefits. In Hankins's sophomore English class at Kickapoo High School in Springfield, Missouri, students learn essential twenty-first-century skills of working together and training in equal participation—in a format that allows each one to receive useful feedback on success and need for improvement. Hankins says, "If we don't prepare our students to work in teams, we are selling them short."

A likely assignment on Shakespeare's *Julius Caesar* is for a group of students to create a newspaper based on the play—news, fashion, sports, weather, op-ed, obituaries ("Everybody in *Julius Caesar* dies," notes Hankins). The students work together on assembling a cohesive newspaper and on design, layout, artwork, and even the paper's name (*Roman Times* and *Toga Tattler* are favorites). But Hankins keeps track—through different colored pens, bylines and other means—of the work each individual student contributes.

In the seven years she's used cooperative learning, Hankins has seen that a full class participates rather than the one high-achiever who always gets a hand up first, and that students get more excited about the work "because the most important relationships that help with learning are student-to-student and student-to-teacher." Hankins is so impressed with the results of cooperative learning that if told she could not use it in her classroom, "I would go sign up and be a greeter at Wal-Mart."

6. CLASS-SIZE REDUCTION

Classes with sixteen rather than twenty-eight students "give us time to get to each student," says Marsha Fritz, a second-grade teacher at Webster Stanley Elementary School in

Oshkosh, Wisconsin. "You can be more specific with each child and pick out exactly what they need to achieve." Webster Stanley is a participant in Wisconsin's Student Achievement Guarantee in Education (SAGE) class-size reduction plan. SAGE provides state funding to help reduce class size to a student-teacher ratio of 15:1 in kindergarten through third grade in schools with large concentrations of children from low-income families.

For three years in a row, University of Wisconsin researchers found that students of all races and socioeconomic levels in SAGE schools outperformed students in comparison schools in all three grades, even when SAGE students started out the school year behind their peers in comparison schools. Another research study found less bullying at SAGE schools.

Students of all races and socioeconomic levels in SAGE schools outperformed students in comparison schools.

Fritz says she sees these positive academic results in her classroom. For example, when second graders in non-Sage schools were given ten minutes to write as many words as they could from memory, they averaged forty-two words. Fritz's students averaged sixty words. Besides giving her students more individual attention, she can give their families attention, too. And when there is frequent communication with parents, they participate more in their children's education and provide information about their youngsters' special needs and interests. "You get to know grandparents. You know whether they have a cat or dog," all of which helps her tailor her instruction to the individual child. Class-size reduction, Fritz declares, "does make a difference."

7. TEAM TEACHING

Tina Prary and Beth Henry started team teaching out of necessity, but they kept up the practice because of the benefits to them and their students. Nevada's answer to mandated class-size reduction and absence of extra classrooms was to pair two teachers in a class of thirty-two, thus cutting the student-teacher ratio to 16:1. Prary and Henry were drawn to each other because of similar discipline styles and educational philosophies.

After six years of teaching a second-grade class together, they like the camaraderie and the practicalities of sharing a classroom. Unlike some team teachers, Prary and Henry, who teach at Agnes Risley Elementary School in Sparks, do not specialize in particular subjects. They each teach all subjects with a system so polished that when one teacher is instructing the whole class and the other teacher feels she has something to contribute, she politely breaks in and adds her two cents. They organize reading and math into two groups, but otherwise all students are taught together. When one teacher is teaching the whole class, the other teacher can provide individual attention to a student or a small group of students—either for academic or discipline reasons—or can attend to paperwork or other school matters.

> Young students see how adults can treat each other respectfully.

These teachers enjoy not suffering the isolation of many teachers and having another adult to chuckle over something or commiserate with. In addition, they appreciate each other's feedback on lesson plans, educational theory and research, and individual student weaknesses or strengths. And they believe they provide good examples for their young students of how adults can treat each other respectfully. As Henry says, "It's like a marriage."

8. LOOPING

At Sherman Oaks Community Charter School in San Jose, California, the practice of *looping*—teachers' staying with the same students for two or more years—helps not only to smooth the bumps of each new year but to build positive relationships between teachers and students throughout the year. After two or three years with the same group of students, the teacher loops back down to start the process again. At her previous school, Principal Peggy Bryan tracked the progress of classes with and without looping and found that student gains were greater in looped classes.

So when Bryan and several teachers from that school came to Sherman Oaks, they brought looping with them. They feel more than vindicated in their decision. Because teachers and students don't lose weeks at the start of school getting to know each other, "students know what your procedures are and you know what their learning styles are, so day one, you're off and running," says teacher Sandra Villarreal-Sweeney. The relationship with the students' families also is stronger with looping, adds teacher Osvaldo Rubio.

> **Student gains were greater in looped classes.**

9. BLOCK SCHEDULING

Test scores are up and discipline referrals are down at Space Coast Middle School in Cocoa, Florida. Assistant Vice Principal Timothy Hurd attributes much of the good news at Space Coast, which gets its name from the nearby Kennedy Space Center, to block scheduling. Instead of six forty-seven-minute class periods, the school now offers four ninety-minute periods, which include two core courses (one in math or science, the other in English or social studies) plus two electives. Because of the longer class time, students receive a more comprehensive lesson that often includes engaging hands-on learning, such as going outside and measuring the building for a unit on weights and measures, or putting on a play.

The forty-seven-minute period led to traditional lectures and students' passively taking notes, Hurd says, which didn't keep students interested and forced teachers to truncate lessons that could have used more time. Student failure rates decreased from 13 percent to 5 percent after block scheduling was instituted in 1996. The percentage of students on the honor roll increased by 10 percent. Test scores increased by 12 percent on the Florida Comprehensive Assessment Test. An added benefit includes fewer discipline problems because less time is spent in the halls moving from class to class. And because students don't take math and science or English and social studies in the same semester, extra books allow students to have a set in the classroom and a set at home.

10. SCHOOLS WITHIN SCHOOLS

Patterson High School Principal Laura D'Anna is a believer in breaking up large high schools into smaller academies. "I've seen the improvements we've been able to make in attendance, achievement, and the dropout rate," says the Baltimore educator. In 1995, Patterson, with a student population of about 2,000, was reorganized into five academies of 350 to 400 students: the "success academy" for freshmen plus academies in arts and humanities, business and finance, health and human services, transportation and technology, and sports. Each academy has its own assistant principal and secretary as well as teachers for programs such as pharmacy technician or consumer services management. D'Anna also beefed up the college preparatory program, adding Advanced Placement classes and encouraging students to take more language and advanced math.

The academies, she says, meet students' requirements for a relevant curriculum with the potential to land them a job right out of high school or send them to college. Equally important are high expectations and the supportive environment created by being a member of a smaller learning community—each with different colored uniforms and teachers who stay with the same students for three years. "Kids have to feel like they belong," D'Anna says. "The teachers know these kids. They mentor them. They're there for them in good times and bad." An overall increase in the percentage of Patterson students passing the Maryland Functional Test, including a jump in math scores from 36 percent in 1993 to 63 percent in 2000, is one confirmation of D'Anna's belief in the schools-within-schools concept. In addition, the dropout rate fell to an all-time low of 1.8 percent.

11. SCHOOL TEAMS

To value each individual student, build group cohesion, and ensure that students don't fall through the cracks, Benjamin Franklin Middle School in Ridgewood, New Jersey, divides its student population into two houses, each with its own administrator. Each house has about three hundred students, who are further grouped by grade (sixth, seventh, and eighth) into teams of a hundred. The student teams are housed in the same area of the school and are paired with a faculty team consisting of English, math, science, and social studies teachers plus a learning specialist and counselor. The faculty and student teams spend the year together, both in classes and in a variety of school activities. Parent conferences include all of a student's faculty team. "It's a great way of getting a sense of who your kids are," says Principal Tony Bencivenga. Lunch hours are arranged so that faculty team members roam the cafeteria and make themselves available to their student team members on a more informal basis.

12. COMMUNITY SERVICE

"What we're here for," says Hudson Public Schools Superintendent Sheldon Berman, "is to help young people develop skills and commitments so they can create a more just, sustainable, and peaceful world. If we simply look at test scores and don't think about ethics and people's ability to contribute to others, we've lost some of the basic building blocks of helping people understand the common good and what our democracy's about."

The Massachusetts educator backs up his words by having every teacher—from kindergarten through high school—integrate service learning into the curriculum. Kindergartners take part in an integrated language arts and math project to produce a quilt and books for homeless women and children. Fourth graders target their yearlong environmental science study to protecting local wetlands. Ninth graders develop individual projects to assist the community, such as a workshop for fifth graders about the dangers of stereotypes. "When young people are involved in making a difference to the world at large," Berman points out, "their participation continues far into the future."

Social/Emotional Learning

Episodes of school violence have focused attention on the social and emotional needs of students, but often lead people to look for quick fix solutions. But the real solutions don't lie in equipping schools with metal detectors. Ultimately, schools, families, and other social institutions need to help students develop their "emotional intelligence," the long-term skills to manage their emotions, resolve conflict nonviolently, and respect differences. School programs that teach emotional intelligence can lead to reduced violence and aggression, higher academic achievement and test scores, and improved ability to function in schools, the workplace, and as global citizens.

The stories in this section include a commentary by Dr. Daniel Goleman, who popularized the term *emotional intelligence* in his best-selling book of that name. Examples of schools and programs where students learn respect, communication skills, and taking responsibility for their own actions are described, including Principal Tony Bencivenga's middle school, where creating a daily television show about the school helps students learn to work together.

Here are some suggestions for "action steps" parents, educators, and policymakers can take to implement social and emotional learning programs in local schools:

What parents can do:

- At home, strive to create an environment of trust, respect, and support through open conversations with your child. Model "emotional intelligence" with your child and others.

- At school, work with other members of your school community to create a climate that supports social and emotional learning—in and out of the classroom. Introduce these concepts at meetings of PTAs or school site councils.

What educators can do:

- Model "emotional intelligence" in your communication and relationships with students, faculty, and colleagues.

- Institute regular classroom practices that support building community and valuing each individual student, such as the morning meetings and journal writing described in these stories.

What policymakers can do:

- Recognize the link between social and emotional learning in schools and student achievement (see the resources at the end of this book for a starting place).

- Visit schools that have instituted social and emotional learning programs so you will make informed decisions about including such practices in other schools.

- Create policies that fund ongoing social and emotional learning programs in schools and the professional development needed for teachers to implement them.

See accompanying
DVD for related
video clip.

An Ounce of Prevention

DIANE CURTIS

Wearing a red paper heart with the words, "I am important," teacher Sarah Button is telling a story to her class of engrossed fifth graders.

Each time she comes to a part of the story in which the protagonist, Maria, is on the receiving end of a deflating put-down ("Get up lazyhead," "You gonna wear those old rags to school?" "What's up with that rat's nest on your head?"), Button tears away a part of the heart. Finally, just a small piece remains.

"How do you think Maria's feeling now if that's what's left of her heart?" Button asks the students, who sit quietly on a blue, green, and yellow rug that is also a map of the United States.

"She felt sad," answers one student.

DEVELOPING EMOTIONAL INTELLIGENCE

Identifying feelings and recognizing the pain of negative comments are elements of a comprehensive effort at Brooklyn's P.S. 15—Patrick Daly Elementary School—to give kids the tools they need to become emotionally intelligent individuals able to move away from feelings and responses that prevent them from getting along with others, solving disputes peacefully, and concentrating on schoolwork.

The school sits in the midst of one of New York's toughest and poorest neighborhoods, the same neighborhood where Principal Patrick Daly, for whom the school was named, was killed in the crossfire of a drug-related gun battle in 1992. But inside the mural-covered, plant-filled K–5 building, where banners repeatedly remind students and teachers of the school motto, "Peace begins with me," children find a haven.

P.S.15 students demonstrate an "I-message" in front of the class.

RESOLVING CONFLICT CREATIVELY

The heart lesson that Button taught is part of the curriculum of Resolving Conflict Creatively Program (RCCP), an initiative of Educators for Social Responsibility which started at Patrick Daly and two other New York City schools in 1985. It has since expanded to more than 385 schools nationwide. RCCP includes regular classroom instruction in violence prevention and social and emotional skills such as empathy, cooperation, negotiation, appropriate expression of feelings, and appreciation of diversity. It also includes professional development for teachers, staff, and administrators, parent training, and peer mediation.

Instruction ranges from "I-messages," the Thomas Gordon-created exercise in which students focus on their own hurt or anger rather than the wickedness of the other person, to role-playing that engages students in finding peaceful solutions. Phrases such as "anger thermometer," "win-win situation," and "conflict deescalator" all relate to specific actions that can be taken to defuse heated disputes and find solutions acceptable to all parties.

The peer mediation program allows students to serve as go-betweens when conflicts erupt in the schoolyard or elsewhere. Peer mediators are trained in such skills as "active listening," which involves paraphrasing what a person has said, clarifying, reflecting, encouraging, and summarizing. The disputing students themselves ask for the mediation and agree to come to a settlement.

A two-year study by Columbia University's National Center for Children in Poverty, which involved five thousand students and three hundred teachers, found that students taught about twenty-five RCCP lessons a year were less aggressive, chose more nonviolent solutions to disputes, and posted better scores on standardized tests than students not exposed to the curriculum.

Students serve as go-betweens when conflicts erupt in the schoolyard.

"We found that an ounce of prevention is worth a pound of metal detectors," J. Lawrence Aber, leader of the study, has said.

Such findings, says RCCP co-founder Linda Lantieri, a former New York City teacher and administrator, should help put to rest the idea that academics suffer when schools address a child's emotional needs. "We're finally learning that it is not an either-or situation," says Lantieri. "Feelings and learning and emotion are all very integral to each other."

While the absence of physical fights is one testament to social and emotional learning at Patrick Daly, Principal Mary Manti says the less easily defined "tone" of the school is different too. "Everyone mentions the tone of this building or the spirit of this building,"

Manti says. "So it's not something that people who are here just notice and live by. It's something everyone seems to feel as soon as they walk in."

See accompanying DVD for related video clip.

A Culture of Caring and Civility

DIANE CURTIS

Although most students at Benjamin Franklin Middle School routinely place above the ninety-fifth percentile on standardized exams, test scores are far from the sole measure of the school's success. Principal Tony Bencivenga believes that turning out good kids who are confident, work well together, treat people with respect, and possess a sense of self-worth is as much a part of his job as pointing them toward the Ivy League.

"I believe that the social/emotional component is clearly the most important of a child's life," says Bencivenga, whose enthusiasm is contagious as he races through the Ridgewood, New Jersey, school corridors calling out greetings and encouragement to teachers and students alike. "If we can create an environment where we feel good and care for each other, everything else falls into place."

SETTING AN ENCOURAGING TONE EACH DAY

Bencivenga's philosophy is shared by teachers and staff and permeates "BF," an immaculate, two-story school in a leafy, well-to-do suburb of New York City. An English class discussion on a novel about the Warsaw Ghetto becomes a conversation about what students can do to combat injustice they witness in their own lives. A journal-writing session first includes a discussion on what it must feel like to be a foster child. A lesson aimed specifically at emotional skills has students naming conflicts that create the most stress for them and ways to abate those conflicts. And teachers working on an interdisciplinary Web project on genocide meet to come up with ways to engage students on a personal, emotional level.

Powerful as such lessons are, the less visible aspect of social and emotional learning at BF is equally as important because it subtly infiltrates every aspect of school life. From the school's television station, BFBN (Benjamin Franklin Broadcast News), a daily student news and public service show produced by eighth graders is broadcast throughout the Ridgewood community on the local cable station. Maurice Elias, Rutgers University psychology professor and creator of a social and emotional learning (SEL) program used at BF, says the television show alone "embodies SEL on multiple levels." The act of producing the show is a community service activity, the work itself requires teamwork, goal-setting, planning, listening, and cooperation, and the content of the programs often addresses positive character development themes.

Students collaborate to produce the daily TV show at Benjamin Franklin Middle School.

The first class period is devoted to building a feeling of community that sets an encouraging tone for the rest of the school day. Period One is used not only to take time to watch the BFBN broadcasts, to go to assemblies and concerts, and listen to special addresses from the principal, it can be the time when teachers invite the students to share experiences or talk about whatever's on their minds or write in their journals. All teachers receive professional development in social and emotional learning and may teach a specific lesson designed to build empathy or cooperative learning skills or community service.

Students at Ben Franklin are divided into two "houses," each with its own house administrator (similar to a vice principal), and then into teams of a hundred. Each team is grouped with seven faculty members, including the four core teachers for that year, a counselor, a learning specialist for students with special needs, and an administrator. The school is configured so that students see their team teachers as much as possible. The full adult team meets regularly with individual students and their parents, which, notes Bencivenga, is "a great way of getting a sense of who your kid is," as opposed to just hearing from one teacher.

Caring and emotional health are as important as academic achievement.

AN EMPHASIS ON COOPERATION AND COMMUNICATION

But it doesn't stop there. The school is filled with small and not-so-small actions that add up to the larger message that caring and emotional health are as important as academic achievement.

For example, no student is denied access to sports teams. "We'll compete with other junior high schools, but the important distinction is we do not have a BF team that seeks to find the best kids who can compete with other kids," explains Bencivenga. During "March Madness," students can win a T-shirt for running a marathon, but they have a month to complete the 26.2-mile challenge. Bencivenga says students who never thought of themselves as athletes have a special feeling of pride when they receive their "I completed a marathon" shirt.

Bencivenga leads meetings with parents, teachers, and students to ask them to define and then commit to social and emotional learning. The administrators use cell phones rather than walkie-talkies to communicate in and around the school because walkie-talkies seem too much like prison equipment. If kids want to come to school early, say at 7 A.M., they are welcome. Most of the time they study in the cafeteria, throw a few hoops before classes begin, or work on a school project. A student store and student bank add to the community feeling.

During the course of a school year, students learn a number of TV production roles.

ADMINISTRATORS WHO TEACH

Administrators teach classes as well as perform their regular administrative duties so that students can see the principal and house administrators as more than authority figures. Counselors stand in the hallways during the break between classes to make themselves available and establish face-to-face contact with students. They also wander through the cafeteria every day.

Every aspect of the organization of Benjamin Franklin Middle School shows students that its adult faculty and staff care deeply about them and are there to guide them in any way needed. As Tony Bencivenga likes to say, "We're here to raise kids."

See accompanying DVD for related video clip.

Reading, Writing, and Social Development

DIANE CURTIS

Walk down a corridor at Wilbur Cross High School in New Haven, Connecticut, and ask a passing student about the "stoplight" exercise. More often than not, a smile of recognition will be the answer. "Oh yeah," the teen will say, "Stop. Calm down. Think. Go."

It's no accident that the drill (red for stop and calm down; yellow for think about the problem and its solution; and green for go with a plan of action) is on the tip of every student's tongue. These kids have been practicing it since kindergarten. The exercise is a recurring element of a comprehensive, districtwide attempt to produce emotionally intelligent students who know how to control impulses and anger, solve problems without resorting to violence, cooperate, behave in class, be self-motivated, and, ultimately, excel in school.

Stop. Calm down.

Think. Go.

A look at the curriculum guide for New Haven's forty-six schools on New Haven's Web site gives a clear idea of the importance the district places on teaching the whole child: First graders "will write stories" in language arts, "will learn about living and non-living things" in science, and "will learn ways to calm down" in social development. Sixth graders will learn to "summarize and analyze texts" in language arts, "describe, model, and classify geometric shapes" in mathematics, and "practice peer pressure resistance skills" in social development.

PRACTICE MAKES PERFECT

"You have to practice it each day like you practice math skills," says Dee Speese-Linehan,

Young students learn simple relaxation breathing techniques.

supervisor of the district's Social Development Department. "Without that constant reinforcement, you don't improve. It's the improvement in those social emotional skills for each individual that makes students more available for learning in other subject areas."

On a recent winter afternoon, Truman Elementary School teacher Mariellen Berrios-Gunn used exercises from a program called Project Charlie and asked her class of first graders to ponder some what-ifs. What if a stranger offered you ice cream in the park? What if your best friend wouldn't let you play with a toy? What if you got pushed out of line in the cafeteria? What if your brand new markers disappeared from your desk?

The earnest, pint-sized thinkers came up with responses aimed at being assertive while avoiding conflict or danger. They frequently referred to their "magic bubbles," imaginary spaces that they set around themselves to avoid entering other people's personal space. They practiced breathing exercises designed to help them calm down, and they identified the feeling associated with a frown or a smile or a red face.

PEER PRESSURE AND HIP HOP

On the other side of town at Cross High School, teacher Sean Woodard guided his freshman social development class through a discussion on overpaid athletes, school reform, the Hip Hop culture, and whether it's realistic to think students can resist peer pressure to have sex and use drugs. (It's difficult but realistic, they decided.)

Teacher Sean Woodward leads his students in a meditation exercise.

He led a three-minute meditation in which the students stared at a dot, took deep breaths, and repeated their common mantra, "I'm as great as I can be." Later, one of the students shared how she had used the stoplight exercise to avoid hitting an opposing player who had deliberately bumped into her at a basketball game the previous night. "I just calmed down and kept my head in the game," she explains. "That is excellent to do that," Woodard responds.

Students bring a lot of "baggage" from their nonschool world "that can sometimes supersede your lesson," he says. "So if students are learning how to deal with emotional difficulties, it's going to make for better classroom learning in every single subject."

An evaluation of the program done by Yale University and the school district found that fewer students are carrying weapons to school, witnessing violent acts, or reporting being victims of violence. More report feeling hopeful. The number of students who go on to postsecondary education has risen and dropout rates have decreased. In addition, youth sex, drug use, drinking, and smoking have decreased. On the academic front, both SAT scores and the Connecticut Mastery Test scores have risen, and the district is in the process of determining the link between the socialization classes and academic progress.

"You don't just teach desks and chairs," sums up Cross teacher Woodard. "You teach people. Every class has to have some social development."

You don't just teach

desks and chairs.

You teach people.

Emotional Intelligence

Five Years Later

DANIEL GOLEMAN

- At a middle school in Puerto Rico, students work in teams on science projects. When there's an angry disagreement between two boys on one team, they don't argue or get into a fight, they go to separate parts of the room to calm down before coming back together with another student, a mediator, to resolve the conflict.

- A class of second graders in New Haven starts the morning off in a "feelings circle," where the boys and girls tell how they feel that day, and why. Says one boy, "I'm really happy today. My father said I could have a bike for Christmas." A girl: "My grandma is in the hospital, and I'm sad about it."

- A sixth-grade boy in a California school has a history of getting mad and starting fights. Other kids had started to avoid him. But in his class, he's learned a method called "Keep Calm" that he uses when he feels himself start to lose his cool: he steps into the hallway and thinks about how he can control his reactions, what he really wants, and positive ways to get it.

THE GROWTH OF EI PROGRAMS: FROM A FEW TO HUNDREDS

Each of these classes, in its own way, offers children valuable lessons in emotional intelligence, the ability to manage feelings and relationships. When I wrote my 1995 book, *Emotional Intelligence,* there were fewer than a half dozen such school programs that I could manage to track down. Today, just five years later, there are hundreds of these programs in tens of thousands of schools—not just throughout the United States but around the world.

The elements of emotional intelligence are crucial for effective living.

When I gave a lecture recently in Shanghai, for instance, I was surprised to hear that sixty schools there were offering children an emotional intelligence–based curriculum. I've heard about many such programs in country after country.

My book, I'm pleased to say, has been one seed for the growth of these programs. My main argument was that the elements of emotional intelligence—being aware of our feelings and handling disruptive emotions well, empathizing with how others feel, and being skillful in handling our relationships—are crucial abilities for effective living. Because data from around the world suggest that these human abilities may be on the decline in children in modern economies, my book proposed we should be teaching the basics of emotional intelligence in schools.

That message alone, however, would not have been enough to drive the spread of these programs worldwide. We have been fortunate to have hundreds of dedicated educators who have taken it upon themselves to develop high-quality curricula in what is now called "social and emotional learning" or SEL—the basic lessons of emotional intelligence in the form of school-based programs.

The best SEL programs teach the full spectrum of EI abilities, from self-awareness to social problem-solving. They repeat the lessons over the full course of a child's school years in a developmentally appropriate way and fit seamlessly into standard curricula in ways that enhance other topics without stealing time from them.

That SEL has flourished owes much to the Collaborative for Academic, Social and Emotional Learning (CASEL), a clearinghouse for quality programs that helps schools around the world identify and implement appropriate curricula. When I co-founded CASEL in 1994 with Eileen Growald, Tim Shriver, and a small group of educators and psychologists, it was based in the Child Studies Center at Yale University. Since then it has moved, with its director, Roger Weissberg, to its present home at the University of Illinois at Chicago. The Web site, http://www.CASEL.org, contains the latest news on social and emotional learning and information on close to two hundred programs available.

The brain centers for emotional regulation continue to take shape throughout the school years.

OUR EXPERIENCES SHAPE OUR BRAINS

The concept of emotional intelligence—and the rationale for SEL—was based on several strands of scientific research. For example, new methods of brain research had revealed that the centers in the brain that regulate emotion continue to grow anatomically into adolescence. And while we once had thought that a child's emotional abilities were largely determined by experiences in the first few years of life, brain researchers were finding that the centers for emotional regulation continued to take shape throughout the school years.

Data also showed that helping children gain abilities in self-awareness, in managing distressing emotions, in empathy, and in relationship skills could act as an inoculation against a range of perils: violence and crime, substance abuse, unwanted pregnancies, eating disorders, and depression, to name just a few.

In the five years since I wrote *Emotional Intelligence,* these scientific discoveries have been supported by new findings. For instance, brain researchers now accept that repeated experiences help shape the brain itself and that this "neural plasticity" continues throughout life. Childhood experiences have special potency in this process. This means that the school years are a neurological window of opportunity, a chance to ensure that all children will get the right experiences to help them flourish in their jobs and careers, as mothers and fathers, husbands and wives, as citizens of our communities.

The school years are a neurological window of opportunity.

The sobering reality of the shootings at Columbine High School and the string of related tragedies in our schools highlights the need for us to offer this education of the emotions to our nation's children. I think of the words of the Renaissance humanist, Erasmus, who wrote centuries ago, "The best hope of a nation lies in the proper education of its children." His words ring ever more true today.

Related Web site: www.CASEL.org

See accompanying
DVD for related
video clip.

Assessment

Traditionally, student knowledge in schools has been assessed by grades and multiple-choice achievement tests. However, reports from some assessments, such as annual achievement tests, do not offer special help to educators to diagnose weaknesses and improve teaching and learning. Multiple-choice quizzes and tests often measure a superficial level of information that requires only memorization but is soon forgotten. Superficial forms of assessment tend to lead to superficial forms of teaching and learning.

The real goal of assessment should be to improve deep and meaningful student learning. Alternative methods such as student portfolios, oral presentations, multimedia presentations, and review by experts and peers can improve documentation and understanding of student learning and provide more detailed feedback to teachers and students. These methods provide a much more complete and continuous picture of student learning, helping teachers and students to monitor their own progress, and modeling the ways adults improve performance in the workplace.

The stories that follow provide examples of alternative, and more authentic, forms of assessment as illustrated by Eeva Reeder's geometry class in Washington state and by practices at Urban High School in New York City. Dr. Bruce Alberts, president of the National Academy of Sciences, comments about assessment practices in science education and a leading assessment expert, Dr. Grant Wiggins, proposes new approaches to a statewide assessment system.

Here are some "next steps" parents, educators, and policymakers can take:

What parents can do:

- Become familiar with the kinds of assessments used at your child's school, and whether and how the results are used to improve your child's performance.

- Offer to assist as an expert or review committee member for alternative assessment of student projects.

- Advocate with other parents for assessment that promotes deeper student learning and engagement.

What educators can do:

- Analyze the forms of assessment used in your school and district. Consider how each type of assessment contributes to improving teaching and learning, such as how, when, and to whom results are communicated.

- Advocate for assessment strategies tied to curriculum and instruction that measure a fuller range of student abilities and provide ongoing feedback for improvement.

- Consider having student projects assessed by parents and other members of the community with expertise in particular subject areas.

- Invite policymakers to exhibition nights or other activities in which students demonstrate their knowledge and skills in ways other than measured on standardized tests.

What policymakers can do:

- Analyze the types of learning measured by current assessments used in local districts and states.

- Consider whether these assessments encourage in-depth knowledge and thinking—or memorization and factual knowledge.

- Become familiar with new forms of assessment that measure deeper forms of student learning and are based on real-world tasks and examples of student work.

- Create policies that include a variety of methods of assessing student learning so that results are fed back to teachers and administrators to improve student achievement.

See accompanying
DVD for related
video clip.

Geometry in the Real World

Students as School Architects

SARA ARMSTRONG

How many windows? What should be done about parking? What are the shapes of the buildings? Can geodesic domes be considered? How will students get from floor to floor?

DESIGNING A SCHOOL FOR THE FUTURE

Every spring at Mountlake Terrace High School near Seattle, Washington, students in Eeva Reeder's geometry classes work feverishly to complete an architectural challenge: design a 2,000-student high school to meet learning needs in the year 2050, fitting it on a given site. As part of the project, students must develop a site plan, a scale model, floor plans, a perspective drawing, a cost estimate, a written proposal, and an oral presentation to local school architects who judge the projects and "award" the contract—all making use of geometric and mathematical concepts and all in about six weeks' time.

Students also maintain a design file, which contains their working drawings, notes, and group contracts such as the Team Operating Agreement (adapted from a similar form at the Boeing Company), in which the team comes to consensus on items such as their expectations of themselves and each other, how decisions will be made, how misunderstandings will be prevented, and how conflicts will be resolved.

Last year's assigned site plan consisted of a beautiful wooded area, a stream, a small hill, and a marshy area; it was designed by junior Chris Armstrong, who had participated in the project as a freshman. Chris also served as the computer-assisted design (CAD) guru for Reeder's students.

CURVED CLASSROOMS AND HOLOGRAPHIC LECTURERS

Teams of two to four students constructed models, researched solar panels and other special features, and talked with visiting architects as they worked to make their dreams become realities. The team of Peter Gudmunson, Devin Lowe, and Amanda Reeves developed a design emphasizing curved spaces instead of the usual rectangular classrooms, more open space and light, underground parking, and energy-efficient features, such as self-darkening windows. Guest lecturers would be brought in via 3-D holograms. While expensive, their design garnered second place.

Team members discuss school structure.

Reeder is passionate about the importance of hands-on, real-life applications of abstract mathematical concepts, as well as the value of experience in working as a team to produce a product. "The ability to work collaboratively is a learned skill. Students need repeated opportunities to practice it within a complex, high-stakes context—similar to what they'll encounter in the community and workplace as adults," says Reeder.

"It may be fairly easy for teachers to create work for groups of students, and it may also be fairly easy for one member of the group to do all the work. That's why the teamwork rubric that students talk about, refine, and sign is key—they define what is expected of each member, and what will happen if a team member is not participating." It must be working. Only those who don't show up fail her class, and she consistently scores the highest retention rate in geometry classes in the Math Department.

> The ability to work collaboratively is a learned skill.

MULTIPLE FORMS OF ASSESSMENT

Assessment of the design projects occurs in several ways. At the beginning of the project, students are given the scoring rubric by which their work will be measured. Each part of the project is evaluated based on quality and accuracy, clarity and presentation, and concept. Reeder also evaluates teamwork (participation, level of involvement, quality of work as a team member) during the course of the project and at the end.

Throughout, she offers feedback and suggestions and meets with the class and each team after the completion of the project. During this final session, the students reflect on their work and what they would do differently to improve. "The longer I teach," she says, "the more I understand the need for reflection— we learn by doing *and* by thinking about what we've done. It's like learning twice when you reflect. It unquestionably deepens understanding, which is always the goal. I want them to keep their learning, after all!"

Sometimes a team will write their reflections, as with one group that never quite came together as a team and didn't score well—an atypical situation for the individuals involved. Each member, however, honestly assessed their contributions and what they'd do next time. "The best part was the next day," Reeder recalls, "when each team member approached me at different times. They actually expressed gratitude to have had the chance to learn these things now, rather than later, when the stakes might be much higher."

> The whole object of schoolwork is attainment and refinement of problem-solving and life skills.

Many forms of assessment determine the grade each student receives. However, Reeder extols the power behind using scoring rubrics as feedback and reflection tools rather than simply ways to assign a grade. "Students are more readily able to separate their personal worth from the quality of their work, and they're able to separate the particular aspects of their work that need improvement from those that don't," she explains. "It demystifies grades, and most importantly, helps students see that the whole object of schoolwork is attainment and refinement of problem-solving and life skills."

PROFESSIONAL ARCHITECTS AS PROJECT JUDGES

At the culmination of the project, each group makes a short oral presentation to the panel of architects, who view the students' work and fill out a scoring sheet. The next day, they review their evaluations with the students during a visit at their downtown Seattle offices. They identify the projects' strengths based on concept, site planning, educational vision, technology use, environmental impact, and teamwork during the presentation. Students also have the opportunity to ask specific questions about their designs and presentation.

Architects Kirk Wise and Mark Miller enjoyed their part in the process. They visited the class several times during the work phase, offering suggestions and answering questions about issues such as the efficacy of solar panels in rainy Seattle and the use of particular building materials in conveying comfort in a learning space.

Wise and Miller donate their time because they recognize the value to students of their insights into a working architect's world. And they have incorporated student ideas into their own school designs. "One student helped us rethink the design of a cafeteria," recalled Wise. "She said we adults worried too much about it—kids just wanted a place to hang out. So we incorporated a café into the space."

A presentation to local architects culminates the project.

The students have their own stories. One girl went home on the first day of the assignment and couldn't sleep, out of excitement about her team's ideas. A boy found his thinking and design skills valued in new ways by his peers. He became a team leader—quite different from his experience in other classes. "This project has been my salvation," he told Reeder. And another girl discovered that an early warning—don't work with your best friends—was a good one. "It got really hard," she said, "to try to get work done. You couldn't tell them what to do without them snapping back at you." For everyone, learning to plan their time to get the tasks done was a challenge at many points.

One of the most thrilling parts of the project happened on the day of the students' visit to the architects' offices. "We heard comments from the architects telling the kids that their work was on par with first-year architecture students at the university—that means a lot to these kids, and it's not something I can say with the same amount of credibility," Reeder recounted. For herself, she says she felt the same sense of pride, similar to what parents must feel, when they let their kids go "and they realize they can make it on their own out there in the real world."

15

Urban Academy

Where Testing Is Anything But Standard

ROBERTA FURGER

To look at Torri Gamble, an articulate, self-possessed high school senior, you'd never guess that the young African American woman struggled through ninth grade.

"I had to get out," Gamble says of her first year in a private New York City high school. "I've always been really opinionated and I couldn't express myself." Before long, Gamble was cutting class and growing increasingly disillusioned with high school in general—and academics in particular. And then a friend told her about the Urban Academy Laboratory High School (Urban, for short), where forming and expressing opinions isn't only encouraged, it's expected. Gamble observed classes, met the staff, and was eventually accepted for admission.

And suddenly school became a place where she could find—rather than stifle—her voice.

"I learned to think about different points of view, to see things from different aspects, instead of just one," says Gamble, a high school senior who is now headed to Howard University in the fall.

But before she receives her high school diploma, Gamble—like every other graduating senior at Urban—must complete a series of academic proficiencies in six key academic areas: literature, science, mathematics, social studies, creative arts, and criticism. These intensive, project-oriented assessments are in addition to whatever tests, papers, and projects students complete as part of their regular coursework. Students typically begin work on their proficiencies in their junior year and must have completed at least one proficiency in order to be considered a senior.

Ann Cook, codirector and teacher at the U.S. Department of Education Blue Ribbon public high school, describes Urban's proficiencies as a system of assessment that measures, over time, what students know and can do. They are the cumulative representation of such skills as analysis, research, and scientific thinking, all of which the students are expected to develop and employ in each of their courses. For Cook and her colleagues, proficiencies are the antithesis of a standardized high school exit exam.

"Proficiencies require students to demonstrate that they can actually do something," says Cook. "They can write research papers. They can devise and conduct and defend an original science experiment. They can apply mathematical concepts to real situations." These are skills, Cook adds, that will serve students well in college and beyond.

A SECOND CHANCE SCHOOL

Unlike most high schools, Urban doesn't have any feeder schools; students rarely enter at the beginning of their freshman year. Instead, like Torri, students transfer to Urban after dropping out, failing out, or being kicked out of public and private high schools throughout the city.

The small school (there are roughly 120 students from all five New York boroughs) is located on the second floor of the Julia Richman Educational Complex, a six-story building that was transformed in the 1990s from a large, failing public high school into a community of six small alternative public schools serving children from infants and toddlers through high schoolers. There's no middle layer of administration at Urban. All of the school's twelve faculty members, including the principal, teach courses and all serve as counselors to their students.

Peer editing and review by mentor teachers helps Urban Academy students improve their writing.

Like the setting itself, classes at Urban are unlike what you'd find at many schools throughout the country. Here, teachers don't lecture or use textbooks as students' primary source of information on everything from algebraic formulas to the Civil Rights movement. Instead, they facilitate discussion groups, create their own curriculum, and from the first day begin to foster in students a commitment to inquiry and a respect for different opinions.

In a constitutional law class, for example, students break into teams that are charged with the task of arguing a case before the Supreme Court. Another group of students serves as the distinguished panel of judges, asking questions, poking holes in arguments, and challenging classmates to use the law, not personal opinions, to defend positions. Attorneys from a Manhattan law firm join in the critique—and the discussion. Their presence provides a real-world connection for students and sends a powerful reminder that student opinions, analysis, and perspective matter.

Outside experts have a part in a great many classes at Urban, and they participate in evaluating every graduation proficiency. A history or science mathematics professor from a nearby college or university may review a final research paper or critique a presentation.

A local theater director may offer a personal critique and suggestions to a student writing a play for a creative arts proficiency.

Torri Gamble's literature proficiency was based on a reading of *Sula,* by Toni Morrison. She discussed it with a mentor teacher, identifying themes, asking questions about interesting or difficult passages, and relating it back to other works of literature. And then, when she felt confident in her understanding of the work, she had a "conversation" with an outside assessor, Sheila Kosoft, who holds a degree in literature and is a Toni Morrison devotee.

Although they'd never met before, Gamble and Kosoft talked for two hours about *Sula.* They talked about the characters. About the conflicts. About being an African American woman. And both learned a great deal from the experience.

"Sheila knows so much. She taught me so much," says Gamble. "She helped me to see things in a way I hadn't seen them before."

Kosoft, for her part, was equally inspired. She says, "I wish someone had done this for me when I was in high school."

SMALL SCHOOLS WITH A BIG VISION

Urban is not alone in its commitment to what is termed performance assessment. It's part of a coalition of thirty-two small public high schools that comprise the New York Performance Standards Consortium. Like Urban, these schools serve diverse students in diverse communities throughout the state. And they share a commitment to providing an individualized approach to teaching, learning, and assessment.

Although their procedures may vary, all consortium schools have adopted a system of assessment that is aligned to state standards and based on a series of well-defined rubrics, so both the student and the teacher clearly understand the criteria upon which work is evaluated. They share a common approach to teaching and learning that is inquiry-based and affords students multiple ways of expressing and exhibiting learning. And they share a commitment to what Dr. Michelle Fine, a professor in the Social/Personality Psychology Program at City University of New York and a member of the Urban Academy Board of Advisors, calls "a culture of mastery and revision."

> You won't see the first draft—these young people understand that you write and you edit and you write and you edit.

"You go in those schools and you'll see mock trials, or you'll see student writing, but you won't see the first draft," notes Fine. "You'll see young people who understand that you write and you edit and you write and you edit. They learn the kind of ethic and intellectual capital associated with persistence, mastery, analysis, and revision."

Such a format takes a tremendous amount of time on the part of students and their teachers. A single paper, for example, may end up being reviewed by several teachers several times before it is considered complete. But the results speak for themselves: Ninety-one percent of all students at Consortium schools are accepted to college, compared to a city-wide average of just 62 percent.

Three of Jane Hirschmann's children have graduated from Urban and a fourth is a current student there. She's seen firsthand the benefits of the school's individualized approach to learning and assessment. From the written narrative and parent-teacher-student conferences at the end of each term to the care that is taken to meet the needs of students with different learning styles, abilities, and previous educational opportunities, Hirschmann is convinced that Urban and the other consortium schools "serve children well."

Teach to the individual child.

"They teach to the individual child," says Hirschmann. "They level the playing field for people who have not had equal access to education before."

And these schools provide students like Torri a much-needed antidote to the impersonal, one-size-fits all education that failed them the first time around.

16

Toward Genuine Accountability

Why Current State Assessments Won't Work, and What They Need

GRANT WIGGINS

Imagine if basketball season ended in a special test, on the last day of the year, in which the players—and coaches—did not know in advance which drills they would be asked to do. Imagine further that they would not know which shots went in the basket until months later. Imagine further that statisticians each year invented a different (and secret) series of such "tests of basketball." Finally, imagine a reporting system in which the coach and players receive the scores—long after the season has ended—without knowing exactly which drills were done well and which were not.

The inevitable then happens (since these new basketball test results would be reported in the newspaper). Coaching becomes distorted in a nervous effort to address the test's form and content. Coaches stop worrying about complex performance (that is, real games) entirely, to concentrate on having students practice drills—at the expense of student engagement and genuine learning.

Who would improve at the game under these conditions? Yet this is what in many states is called accountability of schools when applied to academic standards and state testing. As the analogy suggests, it is really the *illusion* of accountability. Current tests provide woefully sketchy and delayed feedback on tasks that do not reflect real achievement. Current approaches to testing and reporting, in fact, unwittingly cause impoverished, not rich and creative, "teaching to the test items."

State testing often provides only the illusion of accountability.

As a feedback system, our current tests are a failure, in other words, regardless of the needed attention to results and standards they cause.

There is a better way. An assessment system based on common-sense principles about how people improve and are motivated to improve. A more responsive system based on helpful feedback to improve learning. A system that makes local work and teacher judgment more central to state accountability. A system designed to provide incentives for school renewal and built-in professional development each year for *all* teachers. A system that will inspire more creative teaching instead of more fearful compliant behavior.

My blueprint for state assessment would accomplish eight distinct tasks at the heart of genuine (not illusory) accountability:

- Measure student performance against state standards in credible, user-friendly ways, where *how* we test and the content we test has greater fidelity to instructional aims and state standards.

- Provide teachers and students with timely, effective, and helpful feedback, to enable progress toward meeting standards.

- Ensure that teachers of all grade levels and subject areas work as a team to meet standards responsibly and responsively.

- Provide parents with user-friendly and helpful information about how their students are doing now, what the long-term trends are, and how parents can help students improve performance.

- Be minimally intrusive (by not overrelying on time-consuming one-shot tests with no value for current teaching and learning).

- Constantly strengthen and offer incentives for high-quality local student assessment.

- Provide incentives for local districts to continually improve student achievement.

- Enable policymakers at the state and local level to know how students are doing in reference to all the state standards, and have confidence in the results.

A PROPOSED STATE PERFORMANCE SYSTEM

I do not profess to have all the answers about the what and the how. Necessary details await future inquiry, discussion, experimentation, and ownership of the plan by *all* key constituencies. The basic assumption is that local assessment should be a key feature of any statewide accountability plan. The corner-stone of the system would be a *student standards folder,* a collection of evidence in relation to state standards, to be scored against common criteria and performance standards on a yearly basis by regional

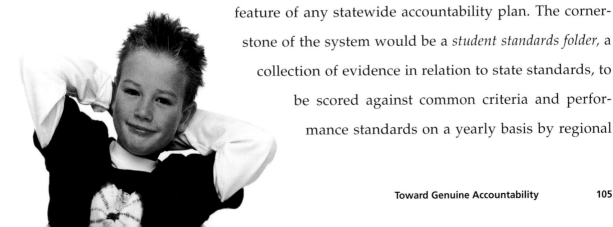

teams of educators. The work contained in the folder would include the following types of information:

- Test data from state standardized tests in literacy and numeracy.

- Test data from district-mandated national standardized tests.

- Results from locally scored state-approved writing prompts and performance assessment tasks. The tasks and prompts would be drawn from a state database of assessments, administered locally by educators at any time during the school year.

- Results from all relevant locally designed assessments.

WHAT IS NEEDED TO MAKE THE SYSTEM WORK

The proposed system requires a very different view of professional responsibility, not only extensive training. The proposed plan—indeed, any plan worthy of being called a *comprehensive* assessment system—can only be realized if the job of teaching is defined as requiring various noncontact days given over explicitly to student assessment, and if school schedules and policies are designed to make such work possible. Rather than thinking of professional development as a series of random days devoted to in-service training, we must redefine the job of teaching to include scoring student work and adjusting teaching in light of analysis of results—for which time is allocated.

The other pressing need is for adequate resources at the state level to ensure that a state Web site offers comprehensive guidance in how the system should operate, a library of user-friendly print and video resources on how to improve assessment, and detailed instructions on how staff can interpret folder results usefully. More generally, the state needs to get more into the business of providing models of exemplary assessment than in merely calling for local districts to figure out local assessment on their own. We need a blue-ribbon committee that represents all major state constituencies to develop the full blueprint for the system I have only sketched here.

UNDERLYING PRINCIPLES OF ANY CREDIBLE AND EFFECTIVE STATE ASSESSMENT SYSTEM

A set of five guiding principles underlie this proposal. These principles serve as useful criteria, in other words, against which the specifics of this system—or any educational assessment system—should be judged:

1. *A good accountability system does more than audit performance, it is deliberately designed to improve performance.* Though commonsensical, this principle exposes the weakness of all current state testing systems. Because the principle implies that students, teachers, and administrators must receive timely, ongoing, and user-friendly feedback in response to credible performance challenges.

Focused and accountable teaching requires ongoing assessment of the core aim of schooling: whether students can wisely use and reflect upon—not just recall—knowledge and apply it in simulations of complex adult intellectual tasks. Only by ensuring that the assessment system models genuine performance, in other words, will student achievement and teaching be improved over time. And only if the assessment system holds all teachers responsible for results (not just the ones exposed to high-stakes testing in four of the twelve years of schooling) can the system improve.

2. *Assessment must be credible if genuine reform is to occur.* Any effective assessment plan must be credible to all key constituencies. It must therefore provide triangulation of local and state data, offering robust and helpful feedback to educators on clearly worthwhile tasks along with intelligible information to laypersons.

Local is better.

Genuine accountability also requires credible assessment tasks—work that more directly reflects the language of the standards and the reality of adult life. More real-world assessment and assessment more faithful to good instruction is key to getting beyond local excuses for test results.

3. *Local is better.* "Trust but verify" must be the motto of an effective state assessment system. Local is better in all walks of life. Standards are always upheld or not at the local level, day in and day out. The state cannot afford to assess each student on all important pieces of work, all year long, nor is it wise for the state to do so. An effective state assessment system thus focuses resources and policy on ensuring that local assessment becomes more sophisticated, rigorous, and self-correcting. That goal is best accomplished by putting more authority, not less, in local hands—while also ensuring that local assessors meet standards for assessment and intervention based on results, and making sure they have incentives to care about state standards and good local assessment.

The proposed system is built on this logic: trust teams of educators regionally with the responsibility of scoring work—for all subject areas. Make results public and framed in terms of standards. Then verify local and regional scoring through a variety of audit systems. Students, teachers, parents, and board members can thus have confidence that the local community will not be surprised by state assessment results.

4. *An effective assessment plan must build local capacity in high-quality assessment, not merely externally test once a year.* An assessment system should improve the quality of local tests, standards, grading, and reporting. Teachers cannot respond in an informed, timely, and effective manner to test results if they are left out of the assessment design and scoring loop.

5. *State accountability must be designed to instigate local creativity and greater local control over standard-upholding, not a fearful compliance mentality.* Two cardinal principles of the Quality movement in business over the past two decades (as articulated by W. Edwards Deming) are "Drive out fear" and "No quotas." The point is to ensure that staff is driven by the right incentives to understand their job is *continuous improvement* and to be rewarded for creative solutions to making progress toward meeting standards.

By contrast, teachers now avoid creative teaching in fear of test score declines. The secrecy at the heart of "secure" testing ensures that dread, not imagination, will drive teaching. By failing to provide genuine incentives for the improvement of local performance, we further promote the ongoing atrophy of site-level accountability and high-quality local assessment.

> Audit testing, applied in a few grades at year's end and using secret tasks, is inherently unable to improve teaching and learning.

The five principles help show why current state accountability tests are insufficient to improve student and teacher performance. Current state plans quite properly put local educators on notice about local performance against state standards. But audit testing, applied in a few grades at year's end and using secret tasks, is inherently unable to improve teaching and learning day in and day out in all classrooms, as my proposal is designed to do and any attempt at fair and comprehensive reform must do.

Related Web site: www.relearning.org

Appropriate Assessments for Reinvigorating Science Education

BRUCE ALBERTS

All of us who work in education should recognize the enormous power of assessments. In my nearly thirty years as a professor, I didn't think enough about this important issue. Although I did see some horrible tests, I tended to dismiss them as inconsequential. I have constructed a little theorem about assessment: "What is measured in high-stakes assessments has a profound effect on human behavior." The corollary is, "We must be exceedingly careful to make sure we measure what counts." We cannot expect major improvements in education without major changes in our assessments of both student and faculty performance.

Due to inertia, our system of math and science education is broken. There is much more inertia in human society than in physics where, if you push on something enough, no

Adapted from a speech to the American Association for Higher Education, 1998.

matter how heavy, it moves a little. However, although talented people have tried to improve our schools, when their projects end, the schools slide back to where they were before. We must all work together to overcome this inertia.

MEMORIZATION IS NOT UNDERSTANDING

Science education should emphasize inquiry-based learning and problem solving that excite and empower children. In this kind of science, classes look different. My favorite classrooms are noisy, with students challenging each other and the teacher acting as a highly skilled coach, not just standing in front spewing out meaningless knowledge to be memorized.

Science is not the memorization of the parts of a flower or becoming familiar with word definitions and facts. Since I am a biologist, let me give an example from seventh-grade biology, which is often a true horror. From one textbook that describes the parts of the cell: "Running through the cell is a network of flat channels called the endoplasmic reticulum. This organelle manufactures, stores, and transports materials." The next paragraph is about the Golgi apparatus, and the textbook continues on like that. Sixteen pages later is an end-of-chapter self-test, which purportedly emphasizes what is important to know. The self-test asks, "Write a sentence that uses the word endoplasmic reticulum correctly."

> Science words are not science.

Science words are not science. By defining science education the way we too often do, we are turning middle school kids off to real learning.

STUDENTS LEARN WHAT IS ASSESSED

For seventeen years, I taught a first-year cell biology and biochemistry course to 150 medical students at the University of California, San Francisco (UCSF). These young people were some of the very best students in America. When I arrived there, all the course tests were multiple-choice exams graded by a Scantron machine. The professors noticed that most students really weren't interested in understanding the material, except for wanting us to be very explicit about what they had to memorize for the exams.

So we created a more complicated multiple-choice exam. The answer could be "all of the above," "a and c," or "none of the above." This new test format was difficult to construct and, after a few years, it had not made much difference.

You have to get the test right if you want to get the learning right.

Finally, we made half of the exam require short essay answers that could not be graded by machine. Immediately, the students' attitudes changed. They had to understand something. It was my first encounter with the real power of tests and how important it is to get the test right if we want to get the learning right.

ASSESSMENT AS INVESTIGATION

Most of the fifty states are now developing their own assessments and their own science standards. Some are quite remarkable. For example, the Maryland School Assessment Program involves a week of testing every year for third, fifth, and eighth graders. Rather than compartmentalizing science, mathematics, reading, and writing, they test for multiple abilities at once.

The following problem was given to all Maryland third graders:

Your teacher has received a bouquet of flowers and is having trouble with them. The leaves are drooping, and the flowers look sick. You decide to do an investigation to discover what might be wrong with them.

Students must then perform the following tasks:

1. Read two articles about plants and their stem system.

2. Write an essay explaining how you would study your teacher's flower to determine what's wrong with it.

3. Draw an illustration that would help other students understand your investigation.

4. With a partner, use a magnifying glass, look at the cut edge of the bottom of a celery stalk [which is used in place of the flower], make a list of things you observe about the stalk, break the stalk, and describe what you see.

5. Put the celery stalk in red dye. Draw and color a picture of what you think will happen to this celery if it sits in the dye overnight. Explain why you think so.

6. On the next day, study the celery that was soaked overnight in the red dye. Write a paragraph to explain how the celery is the same or different from what you predicted yesterday.

7. Write an essay explaining why a scientist might want to do more than one investigation when trying to answer a question about science.

8. Write a note to your teacher telling what you have learned about flowers and how to take care of them.

This kind of assessment stands in stark contrast to most current assessments. This exam tests for abilities that prepare students for the real world and makes school meaningful. With these kinds of questions, parents can appreciate the relevance of school to their children's lives and its importance for getting a skilled job.

HIGHER EDUCATION SETS THE MODEL FOR K–12

Having spent thirty years in universities, I have reached the conclusion that, if anyone is to blame for the state of K–12 science and math education, it's us—the faculty of colleges and universities. We set the standards that define education. If we use multiple-choice exams, everybody else is going to use multiple-choice exams. If we only lecture at students with facts about biology and try to cover all of biology in one year, without teaching anything in depth, our high schools will emulate us. Middle school biology in turn will emulate the high school.

The National Academy of Sciences and its sister organizations are emphasizing improving college courses through a new Center for Education. This work has resulted in an overview publication, *From Analysis to Action: Undergraduate Education in Science, Mathematics, Engineering, and Technology.* We have also published a small book called *Science Teaching Reconsidered* for college science instructors.

On the cover is a photo of a lecture hall that might look very strange. The lecturer is using a technique developed by Eric Mazur at Harvard, which is now spreading around the country. In his large Physics I class, Mazur stops lecturing every fifteen minutes to ask a conceptual question that he knows half the class will get wrong. Students raise their hands to indicate their answers. Neighbors inevitably have different opinions and the students then try to convince their neighbors they are right.

After a noisy discussion for two or three minutes, the students vote again. Now, nearly 85 percent get the answer right. Someone who has just learned something can often explain it better than the professor, to whom it is all too obvious. The technique also keeps the students alert and motivated. Evaluations of student learning prove that it works.

The future of this country depends on *human capital*. If we do not improve our development of human capital in the next twenty or forty years, we will no longer be the leading nation in the world. My favorite quote about education comes from Alfred North Whitehead, nearly eighty years ago:

"The art of education is never easy. To surmount its difficulties, especially those of elementary education, is a task worthy of the highest genius. But when one considers the importance of . . . a nation's young, the broken lives, the defeated hopes, the national failures which result from the frivolous inertia with which it is treated, it is difficult to restrain within oneself a savage rage. A country that does not value trained intelligence is doomed."

PART 2

INVOLVED COMMUNITIES

In the Industrial Age, schools were isolated from the rest of their communities, when the knowledge to be mastered could be contained in textbooks and teachers' lectures at the blackboard. In the Digital Age, most knowledge lies beyond the classroom walls, requiring that the artificial barriers between school and community be dismantled.

Our best schools demonstrate the active involvement of businesses, universities, libraries, museums, science centers, hospitals, parents' groups, and many other types of organizations and institutions. Their partnerships bring a variety of needed resources and expertise to schools. Creating a virtual community through the Internet, these groups are using their Web sites and e-mail systems to provide new forms of content to students and enable classrooms to remain connected to them. These partnerships can serve not only the academic interests of students but the larger needs of children and families, strengthening the entire community.

Through greater community involvement, students see that their learning has a purpose and is used every day in every field of human endeavor. They also see that human and social problems do not divide neatly between mathematics and science and that a study of history can be informed by literature and art.

The involvement of the community enables students to meet and learn from other adults who are passionate about what they do and model positive habits of mind and work.

Involved communities demonstrate that schools and communities have a lot to learn from and to share with each other.

Parent Involvement

Parents, it's been said, are a child's first and most important teachers. There are many ways parents can involve themselves in their children's education, ranging from reading together in the preschool years to helping with homework to volunteering in the classroom and serving on a school site management team. When parents work in partnership with teachers and schools, as "co-educators" for their children, a truly powerful connection is made to support student learning.

The benefits can include increased achievement and self-confidence on the part of students and a closer parent-child bond. Parents also gain a better understanding of the school experience and the challenges schools confront today, as well as a role in developing solutions. The stories in this section include descriptions of model PTA programs, the unusual practice of teachers' making home visits to meet with parents, and the importance of schools welcoming parental participation in all aspects of school life.

Here are some action steps to encourage greater parental involvement in schools:

What parents can do:

- Discuss with teachers how your home environment can support your child's learning.

- Volunteer your time to support your child's school, in the classroom, raising funds, or making connections for the school to local community resources.

- Meet with principals, school board members, and other policymakers to advocate for reforms, such as project-based learning, alternative forms of assessment, and social/emotional learning in the curriculum.

What educators can do:

- Invite parents to play a greater role in the school, through PTA programs and contributing their time and experiences.

- Reach out to parents through increased communication via mail and e-mail.

- Implement a program where teachers call or visit parents at their homes to strengthen the home-school connection.

What policymakers can do:

- Meet with parents and include their voices in hearings to create communitywide efforts for positive school change.

- Include parents as partners on policy committees that implement improved practices for school standards, curriculum, assessment, and professional development of educators.

- Create policies that encourage stronger parental participation in schools and a closer home-school connection.

18

Cultivating Parent Leaders

One School District's Story

ROBERTA FURGER

As a confident Louise Dodson guides a roomful of parents through the steps toward becoming advocates for their children and leaders in their schools, it's hard to believe that just a few years ago she was an angry, frustrated mother struggling to obtain services for her young son.

The transformation from irate parent to school—and school district—leader didn't happen overnight. But through the support of more experienced parents and a school district committed to developing partnerships with all its stakeholders, Dodson developed both the skills and the confidence to stand in front of a packed room and talk about her own journey to parent advocate.

"My son was having problems and it felt like everyone was picking on him," recalls Dodson. In meetings with teachers, everything she and her husband heard about their then–second grader was negative. Dodson knew there had to be a better way to help her son, who had been diagnosed with a learning disability, but she was at a loss as to what to do.

That's when she attended a school PTA meeting and was offered assistance from a parent familiar with the special education program. With this experienced parent to guide her, Dodson soon learned how to be an advocate for her child. She worked closely with school staff to understand the most appropriate services and classroom placement. And little by little, Dodson grew more comfortable with the system and her role in it. As her confidence grew, she began attending parent education courses offered both locally and through the Los Angeles County Office of Education, always with the support and encouragement of her school principal.

Hundreds of parents are learning how to become partners in their child's education.

Today, Dodson is a leader in the ABC Unified School District, a diverse Southern California district encompassing the cities of Artesia, Cerritos, and Hawaiian Gardens, as well as portions of Lakewood, Long Beach, and Norwalk. She's been a member of her local school site council, the PTA board, and the school board advisory committee. She advocates for healthy and safe school buildings and programs for troubled youth. She is a facilitator for the district's parent education programs and served as a co-chair of the district's Fourth Annual Parent Leadership Conference—a day-long event where hundreds of parents learn how to become partners in their child's education.

"I've seen really dramatic changes in myself and other parents," says Dodson, laughing at her own metamorphosis. Besides making her much more confident in her ability to support her children's education at home, Dodson says the many parenting classes she has attended have enabled her to better support all the students in the ABC Unified School District.

"Without those classes I would be just another angry parent," says Dodson. "I'd still be fighting the system on behalf of my children, but I'd be missing out on the opportunity to help other kids."

THE ABCS OF PARENT INVOLVEMENT

Dodson's story is repeated many times over in the ABC Unified School District, where school district leaders consider parent involvement a top priority. In addition to the annual parent leadership conference, the district sponsors monthly workshops on a wide range of school and parenting issues: from communication skills and anger management to strategies for supporting gifted students and the use of technology to support student achievement. Because of the district's sizable Latino and Asian population, workshops are frequently offered in Spanish, Chinese, and Korean.

> Without parents, we know we can't be successful.

Ely Obillo, director of special projects and services in the district, coordinates ABC's parent education efforts and says it has taken years of hard work to create a culture that expects and promotes a strong, well-informed parent population. "Without parents, we know we can't be successful," says Obillo. "And we're willing to put our money where our mouth is to make it happen."

Besides designing and developing districtwide parent education programs, Obillo works closely with school principals, encouraging them to identify potential parent leaders and inviting them to attend parent education classes. Each school can send ten parents to the annual leadership conference in the spring, as well as send parent-teacher teams throughout the school year to an intensive training program offered by the county office of education titled "Parent Expectations Support Achievement" (PESA).

The members of each parent-teacher team are charged with the responsibility of going back to their local school and serving as facilitators and trainers for others in their school community. In the first year alone, nearly eight hundred parents completed the twelve-hour course. Today, Obillo estimates that more than a thousand parents have participated in PESA training, where they learn communication skills, homework strategies, and the power of positive reinforcement.

BIG INVESTMENTS YIELD BIG PAYOFFS

Paul Gonzales, a principal at Fedde Middle School in the ABC Unified School District, has seen firsthand the power of his district's systemwide support for parent education and involvement. Each year he recruits fifteen to twenty new parents to attend the district's leadership conference and to participate in the L.A. County-sponsored training for parents and teachers. "We're only supposed to send ten," he confesses, "but I always ask for more space."

Beginning in the fall of 2000, Gonzales added one more option for his parent leaders: using state and local funds, Gonzales has arranged to have the Parent Institute offer a curriculum specifically for middle school parents. At a price of $50 per parent, paid by the school, the program isn't cheap. But, says Gonzales, it represents a terrific opportunity to help middle school parents better understand how to support their child at home and at school.

"A lot of parents don't have the training and don't know how to ask the right questions," says Gonzales. "This course will give them those skills." Parents and their children aren't the only beneficiaries of the many parenting workshops and seminars. The greater the parent participation, says Gonzales, the stronger the entire school community.

"Parents no longer feel helpless," Gonzales explains. "They know they are supported and are therefore more comfortable supporting their own children. Everyone feels empowered. Everyone has a role to play."

The greater the

parent participation,

the stronger

the entire

school community.

See accompanying DVD for related video clip.

19

The Many Meanings of Community Involvement

Sherman Oaks Community Charter School

DIANE CURTIS

When Superintendent Marcia Plumleigh gave Principal Peggy Bryan the go-ahead to make a new and different kind of elementary school in San Jose, California, a top priority was to make the school a neighborhood hub "where you could really feel the heartbeat of the community." The diversity of the neighborhood was a strength but also a challenge: about 80 percent of students would come from Latino families from Mexico and other Central and South American countries, and there would also be students from Vietnam, Eritrea, Southeast Asia, and the Middle East. About two-thirds of the students would come from low-income families and speak limited English. Bryan and the first teachers recruited for the 1996 opening of what would become the K–5 Sherman Oaks Community Charter School realized they did not quite know how to begin.

MAKING HOUSE CALLS

So they went to the community itself. Bryan and her colleagues consulted People Acting in Community Together (PACT), a grassroots community organization that tackles local problems. PACT led workshops on how to conduct effective one-on-one home visits and on how to listen and build relationships with parents. Bryan and the teachers then compiled a list of families with children who might transfer to Sherman Oaks, divided the list among themselves, and set out to confer with those families—in person. They visited eighty to ninety families well before the school was constructed.

PARENT WISH LISTS

"People had never been asked to dream, and we listened to them," Bryan says. They listened hard. Parents wanted art and music as part of the curriculum. They wanted technology and computers available beyond school hours, both for their children and themselves. They also wanted easy access to social services. And Spanish-speaking families wanted their children to continue to learn to speak their native language.

Teacher Osvaldo Rubio listens while a student rehearses for the evening's parent presentation.

When Bryan and the teachers had talked to enough families, they regrouped, organized the ideas the parents had put forth, and then consulted the parents again in follow-up workshops. They said, "This is what we heard you say. This is how we're moving to construct the program. How does that look to you?" If parents weren't able to come to the workshops, they were kept informed by newsletter.

When a celebratory rally was held shortly before opening day to outline the school program, parents knew—through conversations and speeches in English, Spanish, and Vietnamese—that their wishes had been heeded.

FROM DREAM TO REALITY

The students got the art and music programs the parents wanted. Computers are readily available—not in isolated laboratories but in common areas around the building. "We don't have a technology lab. . . . You wouldn't have a pencil lab, now would you?" Bryan asks. Kids can get to computers whenever they need them, and parents can come in after school to use them. During a popular four-week training workshop called "Technology for Communication," parents set up free e-mail accounts and learn how to do videoconferencing.

> We don't have a technology lab. . . . You wouldn't have a pencil lab, now would you?

The social services are pervasive. Sherman Oaks has one of the largest food distribution centers in Santa Clara County as well as a full-time family services advocate who makes referrals and does whatever it takes to get children needed assistance, even if it means driving a child to the dentist herself. Bryan and her staff also designed a bilingual immersion program enabling not only Spanish-speaking children but others who would like to learn Spanish to receive instruction in both Spanish and English.

The home visits also gave Bryan and the teachers ideas about school features to serve area children's special needs, such as opening up the classrooms and giving the children space to spread out. The home visits had revealed that many students lived in small, crowded apartments, some with two or more families.

BREAKING DOWN BARRIERS

But the benefits of establishing community relationships go far beyond the tangible. "It breaks down the barrier. It just comes down to two people who want the best for the child," says Sherman Oaks teacher Osvaldo Rubio. "It forms a strong bond between teacher and parent." The children then see the relationship as something special. "It's more friend and friend, not just 'my teacher'. . . . It's more like family," Rubio says.

> The benefits of establishing community relationships go far beyond the tangible.

Rubio's dedication extends to coaching the local soccer team, tutoring after school, making regular home visits, and living in the neighborhood. He knows which kids are on the streets at night, whose parents are struggling with three or four jobs, and whose parents have drug problems, are homeless, or are on welfare.

All Sherman Oaks teachers are committed to strong home-school connections. In addition to home visits and regular consultations, teachers meet individually with parents three times a year and hold a community open house in the fall and two student exhibition evenings each year. Members of the school governance council also contact two families a month, partly to inform but mostly to listen to the concerns and suggestions of family members.

ADULTS WHO CARE

This heavy community involvement contributes to achieving one of Bryan's top priorities for the school—establishing the closest possible relationships with students. "It's not going to sound educational, but it really is," she

says, because learning depends on students' knowing that the adults in their lives care about them.

Bryan believes that the emphasis on parental communication has paid off multiple times, especially when the school experienced bumps in the road. Although designed for 460 students, Sherman Oaks opened with 522. Kindergarten classes had an unmanageable forty to forty-five students. Not happy about the overcrowding, the parents nevertheless "hung in there with us," Bryan recalls. Enrollment eventually declined closer to its original target numbers.

Principal Peggy Bryan greets one of her students.

Just as Bryan has seen the children grow and learn, she has also seen their parents grow and learn. Initially, the concerns most often voiced by parents were about safety in and around the school. As time passed, parents have become more vocal about a broader range of issues, from curriculum issues such as extending bilingual education to middle school to neighborhood revitalization.

Educators should understand that their school "is not a bastion," Bryan contends. "Your job goes beyond the threshold of your school. It always goes back to, 'What can we do to make this community more vibrant?'"

The job goes beyond the threshold of the school.

Making Connections Between Home and School

R O B E R T A   F U R G E R

Some called it a throwaway school. Others considered it a school in peril. As far as first-year principal Carol Sharp was concerned, the Susan B. Anthony School in Sacramento, California, had lost touch with the community. The overwhelming majority of students were performing below grade level, suspensions had peaked at 140 the preceding year, and parents—perhaps the single most important factor in a student's success—had become spectators in their child's education.

That was 1998. Today, the kindergarten-through-sixth-grade school has been transformed. Student achievement has skyrocketed, suspensions have been all but eliminated, and parents are respected partners, not outsiders.

"It's like a dream," says Sharp of the incredible changes that have taken place at the school and in its surrounding community. But it wasn't a dream. The changes, as Sharp and others are quick to note, have come about as the result of hours and hours of hard work on the part of students, educators, and parents. They're the result, says Sharp, of a commitment to building relationships between home and school so that everyone—parents, teachers, and students—can work together toward common goals.

BREAKING DOWN BARRIERS

Walk through the playground or step into a classroom at Susan B. Anthony School and you'll see students from as many as twenty-one different countries, many of whom speak languages other than English. (Sharp likens the school to a "mini–United Nations.") Of the school's roughly 450 students, 69 percent are immigrants from countries in Southeast Asia, including Laos, Thailand, and Vietnam. Roughly 20 percent of the students are African American, and 12 percent are Hispanic. All live in poverty, with 100 percent of the students receiving free or reduced-priced lunches. The average parent has just a sixth-grade education.

> Many parents just needed to be asked. They needed to feel welcome.

"A lot of assumptions were made about why parents didn't come to school," says Sharp. "But in many cases parents just needed to be asked. They needed to feel welcome."

Sandy Smith, director of Sacramento Area Congregations Together (ACT), a local community organization that began working with parents to identify needs and concerns, recalls some of the early meetings in which parents expressed their anger and frustration at having been shut out of the system. "They felt inadequate. They felt like they didn't belong at school. And they blamed themselves for their children's academic failures."

As parents, educators, and ACT staff members continued meeting, all recognized the considerable disconnect between home and school. And then, using a model developed by ACT parent leaders and staff, the teachers at Susan B. Anthony took a simple but radical step in the fall of 1998. Together with teachers at eight other low-performing schools in the Sacramento City School District, the Susan B. Anthony staff began visiting the homes of students. They went in pairs and brought an interpreter, or the school nurse when there were health concerns to be discussed. They spent time getting to know parents, seeing their students in their home environment, and they heard (often for the first time) of the hopes, dreams, and struggles of their families.

Susan B. Anthony principal Carol Strong confers with a parent after a school celebration.

Teachers also used that initial home visit as an opportunity to share information with parents about a schoolwide restructuring effort designed to increase student achievement. "We told the community, 'This is a whole new ball game,'" recalls Sharp. "We let them know what we were doing to support their child and asked what we could do for them to support their family." Each home visit ended with an invitation to come to school to a celebration where Sharp and her staff would talk about a comprehensive plan for school improvement.

The impact of those first house calls was immediate and profound. Two months into the home visit program, six hundred people came to school for a potluck dinner and to hear about the school improvement plan. It was the first of what would be many celebrations of the school's successes.

PARENTS AS PARTNERS

Throughout the city there were parents just like those at Susan B. Anthony who were at a loss as to how to help their children. In 1998 Jocelyn Graves counted herself among the disaffected. Her son Timothy was in fourth grade at Mark Hopkins Elementary when she received word that he was reading at just a second-grade level.

> I learned not to be afraid to ask a teacher questions or to admit that I don't understand something.

"I was devastated," recalls Graves. "How could I not know that my child wasn't reading at grade level? I felt like a failure."

Graves went to a meeting at her school, not really expecting much of anything to change. But the more she and other parents talked about feeling uncomfortable on the school campus, of being intimidated and thinking they weren't educated enough to be full participants in their children's education, the more Graves knew it was time for a change. With the support of Smith and Sacramento ACT, Graves and other parents became champions for home visits.

Like their colleagues at Susan B. Anthony, Mark Hopkins Elementary teachers began visiting the homes of their students in the fall of 1998. Graves remembers the first time a teacher visited her home as though it were yesterday.

"The teacher showed me how to make sure my son was understanding what he was reading by asking questions or asking him to write something about a story," says Graves. As important, she adds, "I learned not to be afraid to ask a teacher questions or to admit that I don't understand something."

As her son has moved on to middle and now high school, Graves continues to advocate for his educational needs. "I don't wait for a teacher to contact me. Now I call teachers and set up appointments when I have questions or need help."

SCALING UP

Throughout the 1998–99 school year, teachers in those first nine Sacramento schools made three thousand home visits. The result was greater parent participation, fewer behavior problems, and continuous improvements on the state-mandated standardized tests.

The program's success wasn't lost on the school district—or the state of California. During the 2000–01 school year, teachers in every school in the Sacramento City School District were participating in the voluntary program. Based on the success of the Sacramento effort, California offered $15 million in grants to school districts throughout the state that were interested in implementing a home visit program. During the 2000–01 school year, four hundred schools embarked on home visits. The funding was made available again for the 2001–02 school year.

Home visits build successful partnerships between parents and teachers.

Graves, for her part, has become an evangelist for the cause. She visits schools throughout California and the country to promote home visits as a means of building successful partnerships between parents and teachers, and she trains teachers who are preparing to embark on a home visit program.

Her message is simple but profound. "We're all teachers," says Graves. "We all have to work together for our kids to achieve."

For more than a decade, researchers have been documenting the many benefits of a communitywide approach to education. A growing body of research supports the effectiveness of community schools in providing children with the support and services they need to thrive—academically and emotionally. By providing services for the entire family—from family reading and math programs to English as a Second Language and adult education classes for parents—community schools create an environment where the entire family is welcome and encouraged to support their children's learning. (The following summary is based on materials prepared by the Children's Aid Society of New York City, http://www.childrensaidsociety.org)

- *Children do better in school when their parents are regularly involved in their education.* Research by Joyce Epstein and colleagues at Johns Hopkins University and by Anne Henderson and others at the Center for Law and Education has shown parental involvement to be a critical factor in children's academic achievement, in helping with homework, monitoring progress, and advocating with teachers.

- *After-school enrichment and learning opportunities lead to academic success and improved relationships with peers.* According to studies by Reginald Clark and Deborah Vandell, among others, students who make better use of nonschool hours, for instance by participating in high-quality after-school programs, do better in school, are better adjusted socially, and get along better with their peers. Enrichment and academic programs (offered both after school and in the summer) are typically an integral part of community schools.

- *Teenagers benefit from community-based youth development programs.* Stanford education professor Milbrey McLaughlin has found that community-based youth development programs (including arts, sports, and community service) have a positive impact on teens' academic performance and social relationships. Participation in such programs also leads to higher education and career aspirations among adolescents.

- *Community schools reduce risk and promote student learning.* Researcher Joy Dryfoos has examined research on reducing risk and promoting resilience among children and adolescents and concluded that the single most effective intervention was the development of schools integrating quality education with health and social services. By coordinating critical services in a central location, community schools minimize bureaucracy and provide students and families with needed academic, health care, and social services.

BEYOND SACRAMENTO

As news of Sacramento's success with home visits has spread, schools and community groups throughout the country are taking up the cause of home visits.

In Kansas City, Missouri, for example, several schools launched home visit programs at the start of the 2001 school year, thanks in large part to training they received from the Kansas City Church Community Organization, a sister-organization of Sacramento's Area Congregations Together.

Brenda Munson, vice principal of Gladstone Elementary School in Kansas City, says her school launched the home visit program to "increase parent participation and to help parents feel like partners in their child's education."

Teachers began visiting the homes of their students before the school year began, and the goal, says Munson, is that each of the school's 640 students receives a home visit before the year is out. Because more than one-third of the students are Spanish-language speakers, interpreters often accompany classroom teachers on home visits.

Just a few months into the program, Munson and her colleagues at Gladstone have already seen noticeable changes in parent participation. The number of classroom volunteers is up, as is attendance at the school's twice-weekly English classes for parents.

"Parents feel more comfortable at school now that we have extended ourselves to them, instead of always requiring that they come to us."

Business Partnerships

Businesses offer many resources and perspectives for improving schools at the local, state, and national level. Working together, schools and businesses can make learning more challenging and relevant for students. Partnerships range from school-to-career programs (which provide students with career exploration opportunities such as job shadowing, internships, and mentoring) to tutoring students on an individual basis to individual professionals offering their expertise in class or on a field trip.

The benefits include increased intellectual and financial resources for schools, meaningful interactions with role models and experts for students, and well-educated, skilled employees for the workplace. Dr. Milton Goldberg of the National Alliance of Business provides an overview of business partnerships, followed by several stories describing specific programs, including an innovative use of the Internet to pair business professionals as "telementors" with students.

Here are a variety of ways in which parents, educators, and policymakers can support business involvement in schools:

What parents can do:

- Become familiar with your employer's policies regarding involvement with local schools, including spending time in classrooms and making donations.

- Acquaint your child's teacher and school with your professional and personal interests and skills as a possible resource for school projects.

What educators can do:

- Become acquainted with the resources, skills, and interests offered by parents and local businesses.

- Include parents and local business representatives in planning and implementing school projects.

- Consider how the business community can play a larger role in school reform at the district or state level.

What policymakers can do:

- Become familiar with many ways in which businesses have become involved with schools across the country.

- Promote a fuller range of business involvement in schools.

- Create policies that encourage stronger business involvement, such as school-to-career programs and others that offer students greater exposure to the world of work and present real-world applications of school subjects.

Supporting Good Schools Is Good Business

MILTON GOLDBERG

The business community cares more than ever before about assuring that every youngster has access to a first-rate education. We must not have enormous gaps in student achievement that essentially disenfranchise large segments of our population. The surest way to create a better future for our nation, and thereby better lives for our citizens, is through improving the quality of education over one's lifetime, wherever and whenever this education takes place and whoever provides it. In all these avenues, we must exploit the wonders of new technology.

There are many levels of business involvement, starting with individual employees who commit their own volunteer time and resources to improving conditions in schools. Businesses are actively involved in their own communities in helping to set policies and practices aimed at raising student performance.

Employers encourage their employees to sit on local school and state boards of education, participate in local coalitions, and offer national leadership. Our former chairman, Edward Rust Jr., chairman and CEO of State Farm Insurance Companies, is a good example of CEO leadership. He commits much of his personal and professional time to education, by running meetings for his managers on education issues, convening education and business leaders, and serving as head of major national business organizations.

> Better-educated workers do lead to a more productive and adaptable workforce, but the ultimate beneficiary is the individual.

DISPELLING CLASSIC MYTHS

There are certain myths about business involvement in education. One is that the business community's involvement with education is motivated by self-interest. While it is true that better-educated workers lead to a more productive and adaptable workforce, the ultimate beneficiary is the individual. Further, good schools mean good communities and a healthier, more civil, and more innovative society.

Another myth is that the most important thing business can do is give money. While substantial corporate contributions continue, providing funds is a lesser aspect of business involvement in education. More than thirteen hundred local and state business-education coalitions around the country are working collegially with educators to improve education in the elementary grades, raise math and science achievement, create centers for teachers' professional development, and exploit new media otherwise unimaginable for schools.

Corporations not only encourage their employees to go into school districts, they also provide summer employment opportunities for teachers. These experiences allow educators to absorb the practices of the workplace, including the values of teamwork and innovation to reorganize classrooms and schools.

THE "INVESTING IN TEACHING" REVOLUTION

The National Alliance of Business focuses solely on improving the quality of education over a lifetime. Our five thousand members include companies of all sizes and industries, their CEOs and senior executives, educators, and business-led coalitions. Three years ago, our board was presented with data on the quality of the teaching force and anticipated changes over the next ten years. Examining the research, business became convinced that the single most powerful factor in improving student performance is the quality of the teacher. Business leaders found reaffirmation from their spouses, aunts, uncles, and children who are teachers. They challenged us to develop a project on improving the quality of the teaching profession.

> The single most powerful factor in improving student performance is the quality of the teacher.

In early 2001, the report "Investing in Teaching" was published by the National Alliance of Business, the Business Roundtable, the National Association of Manufacturers, and the U.S. Chamber of Commerce. It represents the first time the business community has come together to send a unified message on improving teacher quality. The report resulted from a series of forums around the country, chaired by CEOs and university chancellors, such as California State University president Charles Reed. Businesses, teachers' unions, and a focus group of teachers reviewed and commented on report drafts.

The report asserted the need for significant social, financial, and political investments to provide teachers with professional-level development, pay, career opportunities, performance accountability, decision-making flexibility, and portability of credentials and pensions. These elements must be tackled in their entirety and cannot be changed through a piecemeal strategy. The business community stands committed to support these changes.

Every recommendation in the report is based on an existing successful program. In recommending new approaches to teacher compensation, we highlighted a bold experiment developed jointly by the Cincinnati Public Schools and the Cincinnati Federation of Teachers. The compensation plan severs the traditional tie between pay and longevity, providing teachers with five salary categories—apprentice, novice, career, advanced, and accomplished—where increases are based on comprehensive reviews and portfolios of teacher and student work. Salary increases and bonuses can also be earned through National Board certification, graduate degrees, and expertise in areas such as curriculum development, technology, and leadership.

Another success story came from the Seattle Public Schools and the Seattle Education Association. Their program moved budget decisions to the school level, funneled more dollars to local schools, and trained teachers and principals on "budget builder" software to hone their financial skills. The report also has inspired many colleges of education to think seriously about changing policies and procedures to reflect recommendations.

SCHOOL COUNTS

School counts—for college *and* for jobs. To send this message to youngsters, we started a project to encourage businesses to ask for high school transcripts. Starting out with two hundred employers in 1998, the program today has an honor roll of about twenty thousand companies. This project, which has involved college admission officers, corporate human resources managers, and teachers' unions, has led us to advocate for changing the quality of the high school transcript, which typically does not tell enough about a youngster's progress over time.

The traditional transcript is limited to a student's attendance and grades, which can mean different things in different schools. A student's school-to-work experience often does not appear on a transcript, yet it is experience employers should know about. Many students are now acquiring technology skills, which also merit recording for employers. We are currently collecting data about school districts that introduce new kinds of transcripts that document a broad set of student accomplishments.

> New high school transcripts document a broad set of student accomplishments.

The Internet and new digital media offer exciting opportunities to create a richer picture of a student's high school record, such as a portfolio of student work for college admissions and employment. Technology can be used to archive and transmit such records. In this era of technology innovation, business can cooperate with educators to take schools into the Digital Age.

POLICIES THAT COUNT

Another critical interface for business is with government. Business leaders can work to influence local, state, and national government and their education policies. Toward this end, we have helped to put together the Business Coalition for Educational Excellence, which has formulated a set of principles to inform new federal education legislation. Recent education summits have included governors and CEOs from states across the nation.

Employers and employees are parents, too. They want to live and work in communities with good schools because they know that good schools and healthy communities go together. They know that education helps young people become mature adults, caring family members, and effective citizens. As partners in shaping communities, they want to work for the kind of schools that will make a difference—to students and to the country. Because setting and supporting high learning standards can make that kind of difference, the business community welcomes an active role in strengthening standards as a means to improving education.

Related Web site: www.businessroundtable.org

School-to-Work Seen as Route to More Than Just a Job

JOHN GEHRING

In Philadelphia, what started ten years ago with a few students in a manufacturing apprenticeship has today grown to a districtwide school-to-work program in which hundreds of employers work with thousands of students and teachers to provide work-based learning experiences. High school students spend part of their days at medical laboratories, law firms, or banks. Teachers complete "externships" over the summer, spending time at local businesses to learn what skills employers are looking for in workers. With strong backing from education officials and a host of corporate leaders, the 208,000-student district has made school-to-work programs a centerpiece of its school improvement strategy.

"For us, school-to-work became the vehicle for engaging employers in schools and really changing instructional practices," said Mary Jane Clancy, the executive director of the

This article appears as a condensed version, originally published in *Education Week,* April 22, 2001.

education-for-employment office of the Philadelphia public schools. "You can't forget this is about increasing access for students who have not had access. For the first time, our children are sitting in the boardroom—not cleaning the boardroom."

As consensus builds on the need to up the academic ante in America's high schools, school-to-work initiatives are being seen as one way to engage students by making learning more hands-on and relevant. At their best, these programs connect what students learn in their academic subjects with the knowledge and skills they acquire from more career-oriented studies and on-the-job experiences in school-related internships. Though some observers say the approach has not achieved the widespread national success that its supporters would have liked, programs such as Philadelphia's are cited as examples of the significant contribution that work-based learning can make.

> Combining the theoretical and the practical has a lot of exciting potential.

"We should continue to push for alternatives to the very traditional high school classroom that is organized around lectures," said Thomas Bailey, president of the Institute for Education and the Economy in New York City. "School-to-work has been very useful for people to realize that combining the theoretical and the practical has a lot of exciting potential."

Seven years ago, lawmakers in Washington passed bipartisan legislation with the ambitious goal of using school-to-work programs as a catalyst to improve academic standards and expose more students to the demands of the workplace. The initiative drew criticism in some quarters, however, with opponents arguing that it would amount to creating job tracks for students. But advocates saw the potential for bridging the gulf between what was happening in the nation's classrooms and the skills business leaders said graduates were routinely lacking. Hopes were especially high for reaching students from minority groups and poor families, who drop out at higher rates than their white and middle-class peers.

In 1994, President Clinton helped give those efforts greater exposure when he signed the School-to-Work Opportunities Act, which led to federal grants totaling more than $1.6 billion in seed money to support programs that included internships, career academies, and job shadowing. Today, the school-to-work movement has reached a crossroads. With federal funding slated to end, states are working to keep alive local programs that many educators and employers credit with making academics more relevant for students and increasing business involvement in schools.

> With federal funding slated to end, states are working to keep local programs alive.

Last year, twenty-four states introduced legislation related to maintaining school-to-work programs. Of the sixty-two bills introduced in those states, about half passed, according to the Denver-based National Conference of State Legislatures. For the 2001 fiscal year, California gave $2 million toward school-to-work initiatives, Massachusetts earmarked $5 million for workforce learning, and Wisconsin will spend $4 million to support work-based activities for students.

CAREER MOVES

A report released in February by the Institute for Education and the Economy at Teachers College, Columbia University, presented evidence that school-to-work programs help reduce dropout rates, improve students' readiness for college, and get good reviews from teachers and business leaders. The report, "School-to-Work: Making a Difference in Education"—described as the most comprehensive review to date of research examining such programs' impact—analyzes results from more than a hundred studies on school-to-work programs.

Career academies—a thirty-year-old model that entails breaking up large schools into learning communities centered on a workplace theme—have yielded especially strong results. The Manpower Demonstration Research Corporation, a nonprofit research organization in New York City that began a ten-year study of career academies in 1993, has

found so far that 32 percent of academically at-risk students who did not attend a career academy dropped out of high school, compared with a 21 percent dropout rate for career-academy students.

While the latest findings don't show improved test scores for career-academy students, they do suggest that those students are as likely to pursue higher education as students on a more traditional college-prep path. In one case, graduates of a California career academy were 40 percent more likely to enroll in a four-year college than other students in the same school district.

The National Alliance of Business, which works to improve student achievement and workforce competitiveness, has helped set up partnerships between schools and businesses. According to Hans Meeder, who oversees school-to-work programs for the NAB, businesses now often help schools develop curricula that are directly relevant to the workplace. Some computer companies, for example, let high school students earn certification by following programs that feature hands-on training in using technology.

BUILDING ON SUCCESS

In Maryland, the state's school-to-work efforts have been organized under a program called Career Connections, which supports student internships and helps restructure schools around small, career-oriented learning communities. One showcase for the approach is Eleanor Roosevelt High School in Greenbelt, Maryland. For years, the science and technology magnet program at the Prince Georges County school attracted students seeking rigorous academics. But even as the program garnered national attention, administrators knew they weren't reaching many students outside the elite program.

> We wanted to replicate the success we had in the magnet program for all students.

With 3,200 students, the high school is among Maryland's largest, and students outside the magnet program often drifted academically. Today, after nearly a decade of improvement efforts centered around breaking up into smaller academies, the school can boast about more than its island of excellence. The high school has phased in academies in areas including arts and communication, advanced technology, and health and human services. Internships and projects involving such organizations as the National Institutes of Health, the National Aeronautical and Space Administration, and the Smithsonian Institution bring students and teachers into the workplace.

Academy teachers encourage all students to pursue college-track classes. Ten years ago, 874 students were enrolled in Advanced Placement classes in fourteen AP courses. Last year, 1,635 students were enrolled in seventeen AP classes. Of those who took the AP tests, 72 percent posted passing scores. "Instead of patting ourselves on our back, we wanted to replicate the success we had in the magnet program for all students," said Laura Grace, the director of academy programs at the school.

Kathy Oliver, who oversees school-to-work programs for the Maryland education department, said school-to-work programs are an essential element of a strategy to improve academic achievement from kindergarten through graduate school. "This has a lot of momentum in the state," Ms. Oliver said. "It makes learning relevant for students. It answers that question, 'Why am I doing this?'"

High school student learns hospital tasks through the ProTech Boston Private Industry Council program.

Building a Bridge to Science and Technology

ROBERTA FURGER

For thirteen-year-old Stephany, a young Latina from East Oakland, California, seventh grade will always been remembered as a year of "firsts."

It was the first time she built an AM/FM radio or wired a circuit board, the first time she visited the city's preeminent science center, and the first time she was able to explore her love for science in an all-girl setting.

Stephany, a friendly, enthusiastic eighth grader at Frick Middle School, is part of a city-wide effort to provide middle and high school girls with hands-on experiences in science and technology. She's one of nearly two hundred girls participating in Techbridge, an innovative program born of a partnership between Oakland Public Schools, two area universities, and Chabot Space and Science Center, the city's state-of-the-art science and technology education facility. It's one of more than a hundred programs funded by the

National Science Foundation and designed to promote gender equity in science, engineering, and mathematics.

Linda Kekelis, Techbridge project director, describes the goal of the program: "With Techbridge, I wanted girls to see the possibilities that technology has to offer and to feel those possibilities were within their reach." The girls benefit tremendously by these opportunities, says Kekelis, adding that the high-tech industry also benefits from the ideas and enthusiasm that Techbridge girls bring with them.

"YOU HAVE BEEN SELECTED"

In the fall of 2000, word spread throughout nine middle and high schools in Oakland: A new program was starting just for girls. Led by Oakland Public School teachers, the programs would feature hands-on science and technology activities, field trips, role models, and more. Some groups would meet once a week during lunch or after school. At one school, Techbridge became an elective class, with the girls meeting every morning for an hour before the first bell rang. At Frick Middle School, science teachers Ron Bremond and Judy McGinty had interested girls fill out an application form before being admitted to the program. Other schools sent letters home to parents explaining the program or handed out invitations to girls they thought would benefit from the camaraderie and hands-on activities. In each case, says Techbridge Director Linda Kekelis, the goal was to make the girls feel special and to make participating in Techbridge a highly sought-after opportunity.

For Stephany and many of her Techbridge classmates, the girls-only focus immediately made the after-school club attractive. "This was the first club just for girls," explains

Patricia, a quiet African American girl who at times seems uninterested in her regular classes, but excelled at many of the Techbridge activities.

"Patricia took to the circuit board activity like a duck to water," says McGinty, smiling. The activity was led by Mills College computer science professor and Techbridge principal investigator Dr. Ellen Spertus, who worked with the girls for three weeks on the project. "Dr. Ellen was really impressed with Patricia," adds McGinty. "She stuck with the activity, even though it was really difficult for all of the girls—for all of us," she adds quickly, including herself.

A fleeting smile is all Patricia offers to indicate her sense of accomplishment and satisfaction at completing the difficult project. When asked how she felt, she says simply, "Like I'd done a good job."

AN ANTIDOTE FOR PEER PRESSURE

In its 2000 report, "Tech-Savvy: Educating Girls in the New Computer Age," the American Association of University Women Educational Foundation observed that remarkably little has changed since the mid-1980s in girls' attitudes about and interaction with computers and related technology. The authors write, "We face a classroom situation that in many ways seems stuck in time, even as the technology itself races ahead. . . . Girls who behave aggressively in computer-rich settings risk becoming unpopular with boys and girls alike. In this context, a passive response often seems the safest and most rational one."

> We face a classroom situation that in many ways seems stuck in time.

The supportive, encouraging nature of the Techbridge program serves as a much-needed antidote to the pressure many adolescent girls feel to "be cool," which can often mean anything but excelling at science and technology. Techbridge gatherings, says teachers, become a haven, of sorts, where girls can explore their interests—or develop new ones—without worrying about being ridiculed or rushed.

"Techbridge girls are more interested, more motivated, and more willing to stick to long-term projects," says eighth-grade science teacher Dan Fleming, who heads up the Techbridge club at John Swett Elementary School. The reason: In Techbridge, girls are in control of their own learning. They decide what activities to pursue and what topics to explore. And without the pressure of a mixed-gender environment, girls are less worried about conforming to a certain image or being teased when they struggle with an activity or concept.

> **In Techbridge, girls are in control of their own learning.**

Among their many activities, the Techbridge girls at John Swett wrote and produced an educational video on the phases of the moon, launched a campaign to educate the community about the harmful effects of motor oil and lawn fertilizer runoff seeping into San Francisco Bay, and studied the effect of ultraviolet light on plant growth.

Several blocks away at Bret Harte Middle School, Techbridge girls worked with Mills College graduate student Jeri Countryman to design and create their own video games using Stagecast Creator, a point-and-click programming tool. The project gave girls a unique opportunity to fashion a new type of game play—one that focused on "beating the clock" rather than pulverizing an opponent. It also provided the thirteen- and fourteen-year-olds with a firsthand look at the creative and technical sides of software development.

Throughout the city, girls explored a wide range of activities, supplemented with field trips, visits from women in science and high-tech careers, and participation in weekend and summer programs at the Chabot Space and Science Center, often offered for free or reduced prices. In the summer between seventh and eighth grade, Stephany spent two weeks at the Space and Science Center, taking part in a creek restoration project and learning about video production— opportunities she knows wouldn't have been possible without Techbridge. "We went around Chabot filming people," recalls Stephany. "I was a reporter," she adds, laughing as she recalls the "bloopers" her team added to the end of their broadcast.

> "She seemed so real. Not like some brainiac with no people skills."

CHANGING THE FACE OF SCIENCE

For many girls, Techbridge has provided a first-ever opportunity for hands-on exploration of science and technology. But the long-term impact of the program goes beyond a single project or activity.

With the help of women in science and technology, these girls began to develop a new vision of what it means to be a scientist. They began to think beyond the stereotypical male in a white lab coat and associate science with real women, with real lives.

The reflection of one eighth grader after a visit by NASA scientist Dr. Aprille Ericsson-Jackson, an African American, says it all: "What I really liked about Dr. Ericsson-Jackson was that she seemed so real. Not like some brainiac with no people skills."

Through their Techbridge experiences the girls are also reshaping their views of themselves and their peers. In conversation after conversation, teachers point to a change in the Techbridge students. They are growing more self-confident, beginning to speak up in class, and assuming leadership roles in their school.

"It's like we planted a seed when we invited girls to participate in Techbridge," says Frick science teacher McGinty. "Suddenly they believed they had what it took to be a leader."

If Techbridge teachers planted the seed, then the girls themselves nurtured it and helped it to grow. And they created a safe, nurturing place to celebrate their newfound selves.

> "It's not cool to be a girl and smart in this school. But it is in Techbridge."

Every week before the Frick girls begin a new activity, they gather in a circle to check in and talk about their week. McGinty recalls one memorable Friday afternoon when the talk turned to their recently distributed report cards.

"They started talking about grades and they were so proud of one another. Every time one of the girls shared that she got an 'A,' the other girls would cheer and say, 'Hey, that's cool,'" says McGinty. "They even helped each other figure out how they could get a better grade from certain teachers," she adds, "sharing tips like, 'Oh, with him you just need to make sure you turn in all of your homework.'"

For some, the conversation might not seem exceptional, but McGinty knew she was witnessing something very profound—perhaps even life-changing. "It's not cool to be a girl and smart in this school. But it is in Techbridge."

Scientists in Classrooms Make Sense

DIANE CURTIS

Gerry Lewis, a chemical technician, looks out over fifty bright faces at a Pittsburgh school as he blows up a balloon and sticks a wooden skewer into the top of the rubbery orb. Nothing happens, which is exactly what Lewis expects but it's a surprise to the children, who have covered their ears with their hands.

"Polymers," says Lewis, who is wearing a whimsical, tie-dyed lab coat. "Tight polymer strands on the sides. Loose polymer strands on the top and bottom." He explains that polymers are chemical compounds or mixtures consisting of chains of repeating molecules. Some of those chains are formed loosely. Others are close together. The ones that are loose allow a skewer to poke through without bursting the balloon. The children giggle and cheer.

VOLUNTEERING BENEFITS STUDENTS, TEACHERS, AND VOLUNTEERS

Lewis is an emissary from Bayer Corporation's Making Science Make Sense (MSMS), a school-business partnership that shows teachers and students that the best way to learn science is to do science-asking questions, hypothesizing, experimenting, analyzing, and testing. You can see the Making Science Make Sense Web site at www.bayerus.com/msms/about.

The best way to learn science is to do science.

Volunteering "really enriches the way I feel about my job," says Pat Jacobs, a scientist in the coatings and colorant division who also directs the Pittsburgh volunteer effort. "You get so serious here at work working against deadlines. To be able to enjoy science from a child's point of view is really renewing. It makes you appreciate the company more, and I certainly know more about the schools."

Employee volunteers, both scientists and nonscientists, attend "lunch and learns," monthly meetings to teach new experiments and their theories. Volunteers are given time off to work in the schools. Jacobs says many parent volunteers first go into their child's classroom and end up working with three or four others because so many teachers appreciate the hands-on help, the humanizing of science, and the materials that come with the demonstrations.

The Bayer program—involving more than twelve hundred employees at twenty-two locations—is a companywide initiative and has won numerous awards, including the President's Service Award 2000. Programs include a science center at a California school, an environmental awareness program in South Carolina, "farm day" for city kids in Missouri, and a national competition in which middle school students solve community problems through science and technology.

"YOU CHANGED MY SON'S LIFE"

Lewis, one of most popular and busiest of Bayer's volunteers, has almost become a legend in Pittsburgh, having made more than a hundred appearances at schools and other institutions. He and other volunteers tailor their presentations to the curriculum needs of each grade and teacher.

"Kids love science if they realize it's hands-on," says Lewis. "Once you've touched something, you understand it better."

His wide-ranging demonstrations include activity-based lessons on gravity, mixtures, the periodic table, the properties of space, biodegradability, color separation, or static electricity. The heartfelt responses he receives are worth more than the extra hours he puts in. "You changed my son's life," one mother told him. "We wish that one day we

Scientist Gerry Lewis brings hands-on science into schools.

could both be really cool scientists," a boy wrote of himself and his brother. One elementary school principal commented, "Seeing a professional Afro-American male, such as yourself, will inspire the younger generation of Afro-American males to pursue a career in science . . . or another professional field."

Related Web site: www.bayerus.com/msms/about

The Virtual Mentor

Business Professionals Go Online with Students

MILTON CHEN

In Homer's *Odyssey*, Mentor was the teacher in whose care Odysseus left his son, Telemachus, when he set off on his voyages. In its original meaning, a mentor is a teacher. Across the country, many organizations, such as the National Mentoring Partnership and the California Mentor Foundation, are demonstrating the value of mentoring for young people and for adults learning new professions, such as novice teachers. Mentors provide invaluable one-on-one advice, role modeling, training, and encouragement to learners.

"Telementoring" provides a unique virtual space where, for the first time in mentoring history, every student with Internet access can have a mentor. The International Telementor Program (ITP) started in 1995 when David Neils, a software engineer at Hewlett-Packard, created an opportunity for Kruse Elementary School students from Fort Collins, Colorado, to pursue a unique interest in a project-based environment. After four weeks, it became apparent that the only way the students would receive additional mentoring support from HP employees was if the connection was virtual. The employees simply didn't have time to drive miles to and from the school each week. Neils began to use e-mail to make the connection with HP professionals, who were eager to help. The program expanded from one elementary school to include 350 students throughout the United States, Canada, Australia, and Germany.

Telementoring allows every student with Internet access to have a mentor.

"ITP's real focus isn't about technology or even telementoring," says Neils, who has continued as the project's director. "It's about helping students redefine learning where success is measured by how effectively the student is leveraging resources at school and home, in the local community, and globally to pursue unique interests. Grades, GPA, and standardized test results become byproducts rather than the focal point."

PROJECT MANAGEMENT HAPPENS VIRTUALLY

In championing the power of the Internet to put business professionals in close touch with students and teachers, ITP practices what it preaches, using an ingenious Web site to administer the program. ITP uses the Web site to manage teacher and mentor applications, project plans, matching, daily monitoring, and evaluations for each group of students and mentors. It includes project descriptions and needs for specific mentor backgrounds, examples of current and previous projects, and advice to mentors.

The program's success results from self-selected teachers, students, and mentors combined with clear requirements, lightning-fast support, and a personal connection with a dedicated ITP staff member. "Technology simply allows an efficient and productive connection between student and mentor," says Neils.

A CREATIVE APPROACH TO CREATIVE WRITING

For instance, seventh-grade teacher Isaac Burson in Bossier City, Louisiana, designed a semester-long project on creative writing and publishing, whose goal was for students to create, revise, and publish a personal narrative, three poems, and a short story. Mentors with background and interest in creative writing matched themselves with each of Burson's students and, in one of their first assignments, introduced their personal interests and job responsibilities to the students.

E-mail effectively connects students and mentors.

On a weekly basis, mentors not only evaluated student ideas and helped shape their written work into final, polished products but also engaged in a two-way exchange, sharing their own written personal narratives for critique by students. Students and mentors worked together to identify online publishing opportunities for the students' work. The e-mail exchanges between students were published in an online "e-group" space, so that all student-mentor pairs could see the work of all other pairs in the class, encouraging further cross-pollination of ideas. The quality of communication continued to improve throughout the project. Students and mentors were inspired by reading the text of the best mentors and students in the group.

Other recent projects carry titles of "Shakespeare's 'The Tempest,'" "Plant Responses to Stress," "Career Search for Limited English Proficient Students," "California History Multimedia Presentation," "Virtual Math Lab Partner," and "Something Is Wrong in Michigan's Lakes and Ponds!"

WORKING ON INTERNET TIME

The initial mentor matches happen on Internet time. Consider the problem of finding mentors for eighty-seven students involved with seventh-grade teacher Martha Cutright's project on "Developing an Educational Action Plan" in Dodge City, Kansas. Her project was designed to help students identify learning goals they were truly passionate about and develop an educational plan to achieve them. Using ITP's Web site and e-mails to ITP's mentor pool, mentors for each student were found from around the world–in six hours! Neils explains, "Our mentors know that if they don't respond to that e-mail before lunchtime, when they get back, the mentoring opportunity with a particular project and student will probably be snapped up by another mentor. The average time between a submitted mentor application and a student match is six minutes. The average time spent waiting for a mentor in a traditional program is one year."

> The average time between a submitted mentor application and a student match is six minutes. The average time spent waiting for a mentor in a traditional program is one year.

Since 1995, more than eighteen thousand students, teachers, and mentors have participated, including mentors from eight other nations. More than five thousand students will be mentored in this year alone, ranging from fifth through twelfth grades, and some college students, as well. Originally supported by Hewlett-Packard, ITP is now a program of the Keystone Center in Colorado, with sponsorship from HP, Agilent, the Merck Institute for Science Education, Thomson Financial, Sun Microsystems, Cinergy, and others. It provides a cost-effective model for bringing new expertise and energy into the classroom, at a cost of about $2.50 per student each week.

"A PHENOMENAL CONNECTION IN CYBERSPACE"

Maureen Pajak, a teacher at Mayfield Elementary School in Lapeer, Michigan, writes, "What a positive impact this has had in academic as well as social/psychological arenas! When students can't wait to get to school to check the computer for messages from their mentors, compete for time on the keyboard, even giving up recess time to surf the Net to check out Web sites sent by mentors, we've made a phenomenal connection. My pupils know there is at least one other person out there in cyberspace who cares about them and wants to help them achieve success."

Neils sees the purpose of the International Telementor Program as nothing less than connecting students' passions to their studies and to their lives. "There are too many kids whose spark for learning is completely doused by the seventh grade," he says. "When I talk to third and fourth graders about pursuing their dreams, they're excited, animated, and leaning forward. Sixth and seventh graders look puzzled and are sitting up straight. By high school they're sitting back with their arms crossed waiting for the final bell to ring."

"We need systemic changes," Neils points out firmly, "where the focus of our learning environment is to help students leverage resources effectively with their interests as the focal point. We all win if we help our students develop the skills and foundation to pursue their dreams successfully. Telementoring is a powerful dream-launching tool."

Related Web sites: www.telementor.org

Community Partnerships

Partnerships with parent and community groups, nature and science centers, libraries, museums, hospitals, universities, and others can make learning in schools more dynamic and help schools become true centers of learning in their communities. Several innovative partnerships are described here, including Internet projects that link schools globally for community action, community technology centers that provide educational opportunities and technology access, and "community schools" that provide services to address the needs of the whole child.

What parents can do:

- Explore ways in which local community organizations such as museums, as well as colleges and universities, can be included in school programs.

- Invite community groups to attend PTA or school site council meetings to share ideas for improving schools and incorporating community-based activities into the curriculum.

- Consider ways in which schools can expand into community centers to include health care and training for parents and other adults in the community.

What educators can do:

- Encourage stronger community partnerships with local schools.

- Consider how technology can support the involvement of community-based organizations through, for instance, accessing their Web content and experts.

- Encourage community organizations to advocate on behalf of school programs with local, regional, and state policymakers.

- Consider ways in which school buildings and facilities can support community organizations and bring new resources into schools.

What policymakers can do:

- Become familiar with the ways in which community organizations are partnering with schools in your local area as well as nationally.

- Include representatives of community organizations in groups developing educational policies.

- Consider the many ways in which schools can work together with community groups to create stronger communities and address the larger needs of children and families.

- Create policies to encourage school-community partnerships and incentives for schools and community groups to work together.

It Takes Many Villages

The International Education and Resource Network

EDWIN H. GRAGERT

A teacher in Pakistan writes, "Giving our students a global exposure and enhancing their communication skills . . . will make a world of difference to their academic life and interest in the subject."

For this teacher, as for the thousands of other educators involved in the International Education and Resource Network (iEARN), the objective is to prepare students to be motivated, culturally respectful, and active participants in their world.

To meet this objective, iEARN projects make use of an extraordinary technology for worldwide understanding: the World Wide Web. Students in Belarus post their folk tales on the Internet and in turn are treated to student interpretations of local folk tales from around the world, providing a unique window into new cultures, customs, traditions, and beliefs. Middle-school students in Australia research existing conditions about their wetlands, post them on the Internet as part of iEARN's Wetlands Project, and then reap the benefits of similar research done by students in Uganda, the United States, and Romania.

Students involved in a project to clear land mines not only study the deadly remains of war, they are able to talk—via e-mail—with experts in Mozambique and Afghanistan who do the clearing. The students also hear the stories of their peers across the world who must live with land mines. Many then take the next step to raise money or write to policymakers to help end the horrible threat.

SUPPORT ACROSS CONTINENTS

iEARN is a network of teachers and students who use the Internet and e-mail to carry out collaborative projects that embody activist teaching and learning. iEARN educators seek to prepare the youth of today for living in a multicultural and interdependent world that is being redefined every few years as technology and economics change. The need for understanding cultures and religions different from our own has only been heightened by the tragic terrorist attacks on September 11, 2001.

The iEarn Web site includes student projects, teacher resources, and other resources.

In just twelve years of operation, iEARN has linked schools from Tucson, Arizona, to Paramaribo, Suriname, to Novosibirsk, Russia. iEARN currently works with approximately 350,000 students at four thousand schools in more than ninety countries. Twenty-nine languages are represented. Global projects are based on interactive discussions, or forums, in which students and teachers debate, research, and share opinions.

The projects run the gamut: global arts and music, city art videos, environmental action, the power of math, hunger, local birds, flowers and symbols, faces of war, indigenous peoples, the Holocaust and genocide, child labor, world religions, ending violence, international foods and cultural patterns, local history, solstice holidays, democracy in schools, and youth volunteerism and service.

THE IMPORTANCE OF GLOBAL COLLABORATION

Through international collaboration, problems get solved. But the individual student benefits as well. We see heightened motivation in class. We see improved reading and writing skills. We see excited students taking one aspect of a project and expanding it to another that they created on their own.

In just twelve years, iEARN has linked schools from Arizona to Suriname to Russia.

But to create these motivated, internationally aware and connected students requires teachers with the technical skills and support to guide them. iEARN does not dictate what people should do but is a partner working with teachers, both new and experienced, to offer training, curriculum resources, inspiration, and human interaction around areas of mutual interest.

One of the central ideas behind the iEARN network is that by working together we can maximize our potential to enhance the quality of life on the planet. Every activity of iEARN stems from this vision. iEARN projects are intended to improve the health and well-being of the world through collaboration. All aspects, from curriculum projects to professional development workshops, build on collaborative approaches.

For example, iEARN educators developed three- and five-day sets of workshops for a World Bank program called "WorLD" (World Links for Development). The workshops, titled "It Takes Many Villages to Make the World: Honoring People and Learning," emphasize community building, respect for others, and a focus on methods by which teachers can empower students to use technology to make a difference in their lives and the lives of the six billion inhabitants of the planet.

In the first session of the program, typical of the kinds of approaches used throughout, each participant learns a different skill, such as bookmarking on the Web, and then teaches that skill to another participant, creating a "community of learners." They go on to learn about integrating curriculum into their classrooms, but the methods of learning remain collaborative and the focus is on learning the technology for what it can accomplish with students.

TECHNOLOGY IS NOT AN END IN ITSELF

There is an ocean of difference between a workshop whose purpose is to familiarize teachers with a particular piece of software or hardware and one that teaches educators to use technology to prepare students to address racism or school conflict. Changing the focus of professional development to teaching and learning with a community purpose is only the first step. The next and ongoing component is interactive support when teachers return to their schools and their own computers. As the research of University of California education professor Hank Becker and others has shown, less than 10 percent of teachers with access to technology actually engage in collaborative projects.

Significant support is imperative. Toward this end, newly trained iEARN teachers are immediately able to interact meaningfully with peers through online support communities. This support structure is sustainable because responsibility for it rests primarily in the hands of the teachers themselves.

We realize that to take professional development to scale and across geographic boundaries, it will be necessary to supplement face-to-face workshops with Internet-based courses on how to integrate project-based learning in classes. Initial courses are now available—enabling teachers from around the world to experience global interaction among peers as they learn to navigate the Web, online discussion forums, and global issues involving their students—all within a context of the curriculum and educational standards in which teachers work each day.

IT WON'T BE EASY

But much more must be done, as evidenced by complaints from students who move from a school in which global interaction is an integral part of the academic program to one in which it is not. Young men and women write back to us from college and say, "We're so disappointed. We got to college, and they don't even interact with native speakers in my Spanish class. In high school in iEARN, that's all we did."

The goal of iEARN is to have people go to the source in dealing with the problems they face—locally, regionally, nationally, and internationally. If iEARN students learn as children that they can go directly to real people in China to find out about an issue, they will carry that knowledge with them to adulthood. They won't rely on a thirty-second sound bite when they hear about a crisis on the other side of the world. They will be encouraged to think collaboration, not confrontation.

iEARN students think collaboration, not confrontation.

People, languages, cultures, and social structures in this global environment are in constant interaction. It is our hope that an increase in collaboration will result in a lessening of ignorance about other cultures and a reduction in global conflict. As global educators, our purpose is to nurture the powerful curiosity and natural enthusiasm that all young people have for learning about the world around them.

Related Web site: www.iearn.org

LEARNING BECOMES "INTERNET-IONAL"

Projects developed and implemented by iEARN teachers and students cover a wide range of topics, including Aspects of Love, the Bullying Project, Celebrating Our Women, Child Soldier Project, Connecting Math to Our Lives, Everyday Superstitions, Faces of War, Joys of Music, Local Birds and Tales about Birds, Medicine in My Backyard, Solar Cooking Project, and Youth CaN. Descriptions of others follow. See http://www.iearn.org/projects for a full listing of current iEARN projects.

If Rocks Could Talk . . . What Would They Tell Us?

This project promotes students' analysis and study of their environment and shares their experiences with students from other geographical regions. Students collect, classify, and analyze different types of rocks and their surrounding environment in rock quarries and other areas in the community. This information is shared through e-mail exchanges. Students also create packages they send through the mail, including local cultural artifacts.

First Peoples Project

The project links indigenous students around the world with an exchange of ideas, cultures, and art in both English and Spanish. People from indigenous groups in Argentina, Australia, the United States, Hungary, Thailand, Mexico, and Guatemala are currently involved. Three components include the Indigenous Global Art Exchange, the Writing Project, and the First Peoples' Humanitarian Effort.

Planetary Notions

Planetary Notions is an environmental project in which students publish articles in an annual magazine to share their views about the world's environmental health and how to better protect it. The project facilitates discussion about these issues through an online forum that also gathers articles on environmental subjects. The publication includes summaries of some of the major discussions from the year.

The Value of Money

Participants consider the role of money in societies and examine how to earn money through arts, crafts, or other skills. The project includes writing essays and poems, taking pictures, playing virtual games, and handling real money. Participants also exchange items with their friends using a barter system. Action projects are included to spread awareness about budgeting money, as well as using it wisely and in socially responsible ways.

Laws of Life Essay Project

"Laws of life" are the rules, ideals, and principles by which one chooses to live. The Laws of Life Project invites young people to express what they value most in life in their own words through essays about their own laws of life. Participants respond to each other's essays through e-mail and are encouraged to use what they learn about values to initiate change within their own community through action projects. A book of essays is published each year.

"Super Hero" Cartoon Art

Students develop and create their own cartoons or comic strips that relate to a character of "super hero" status, who always does something good for the environment or humanity. Students produce and distribute a book that is both funny and serious.

27

Back to Class for School Board Members

DIANE CURTIS

Shortly after the exhilaration of political victory gives way to appreciation of the daunting task before them, all new school board members in West Virginia become students. Classes are mandatory and include such subjects as school budgeting, conflict-of-interest laws, federal and state authority over education, and how to run a meeting. Since our nation's fifteen thousand school boards and ninety-five thousand school board members provide critical local governance, well-prepared school board members are essential. "Because we have these programs, we enhance board members' ability to provide better leadership," says Suzie Cvechko, president of the West Virginia School Boards Association.

MANDATED SCHOOL BOARD TRAINING

Following the lead of states like Georgia and Texas, in 1990 West Virginia lawmakers passed a bill requiring school board members to receive instruction on education issues and management techniques pertinent to their office. Howard O'Cull, executive director of the association, says the bill was preceded by a state study showing that although school boards' primary responsibility was to set policy, only 3 percent of their efforts were in that area. An outside advisory group also concluded that school boards spent too much time in day-to-day operations.

The West Virginia orientation typically provides a grounding in school finance and education law, including information on state and federal versus local responsibilities. It offers advice on how to run a board meeting (including a detailed seminar on Robert's Rules of Order) and communication tips on dealing with the public, the media, the superintendent—and each other.

Sessions on financing have been especially helpful, Cvechko says, noting that school board members "come from all walks of life." Most, she adds, "are not educators." Cvechko, who attended the first orientation in 1992, says one of the early eye-openers was learning how little discretionary money is in a school district budget. But every year provides new information, often relating to that year's hot topic, such as violence or religion in the schools.

In West Virginia, the three-day orientation occurs shortly after the May elections for new board members and those who may have had a break in service. The trustees are also required to receive at least another seven hours of additional training for every year they are in office. Cvechko is one of the many school board members who routinely exceeds the seven-hour requirement.

The additional training programs, which take place at least twice a year, focus on a main theme such as school safety, special education, religion in the schools, or board-superintendent relations. Some have been held through videoconferences to minimize the time and expense of travel.

GROWING INTEREST IN OTHER STATES

More than a dozen states now require school board members to attend seminars, lectures, or conferences, either yearly or over the course of their time in office. Many states do not mandate training but encourage it as a way to get a better understanding of the varied and often complicated issues that dominate school board agendas—from deciphering low state test scores to meeting the technology needs of students and dealing with a more violent society.

A number of school board organizations balk at the idea of mandatory training because of opposition to state requirements that don't come with funding or because they don't believe school board members should be singled out for instruction not required of other elected representatives. But most agree that school board members can benefit from a deeper knowledge of the duties of their office and education issues.

TECHNOLOGY-SAVVY SCHOOL BOARD MEMBERS

Cvechko and others also greatly value the collegiality of the seminars. The networking continues long past the time of the face-to-face meetings, thanks to former association President David Kurtz.

When he was a board member in Wood County, Kurtz started a personal Web site that included a vast amount of school board and education information as well as two e-mail discussion groups. One discussion group was for anyone interested in Wood County education and another was exclusively for West Virginia school board members—"where we let our hair down," Kurtz says.

A school board member from the eastern panhandle could throw out a problem that might resonate with someone at the other end of the state who might be able to offer a solution. Board members were not limited by the time constraints of scheduled meetings only two or three times a year. They could log onto the Internet anytime day or night and expect responses almost immediately. "One person sharing his thoughts on a particular issue helps enlighten board members all across the state," says Kurtz.

West Virginia Wood County school board member Judy Sjostedt found mandatory classes beneficial.

In 2001, the West Virginia School Boards Association took over hosting the discussion group, which Executive Director O'Cull says generated about fifteen messages a day and has proved its worth. "It brought people together outside the context of a meeting where they physically had to drive someplace. It brought to their attention that other people had the same problems and situations. It's also good for passing information on the unity of school boards and school board perspective on issues," he says.

THE VALUE OF E-MAIL AND WEB PAGES

School board leadership must include technology, believes Kurtz. "I really think that the idea of school board members helping to bridge that gap between the school and community by e-mailing and Web pages and discussion groups really is the wave of the future," he says. "It's part of the changes that our democracy needs to make to better represent our constituencies and to advocate on behalf of school issues."

And O'Cull adds that the age-old benefits don't get lost in the technological wizardry. "We never took away the grassroots vision."

28

The Whitefoord Community

Bringing Schools and Services Together

ROBERTA FURGER

Audrey Smith has seen a lot of well-intentioned programs come and go in Whitefoord, a small, predominantly African American community in Atlanta, Georgia. And too often, she says, the programs have been based on someone else's idea of what the poor, largely underserved neighborhood needed.

"Many people have promised us the world and then didn't give us anything but a few raindrops to wet our lips," says Smith, who is a family advocate and member of the Whitefoord Community Advisory Council.

But since 1995, the Whitefoord Community Program, a neighborhood-based not-for-profit organization, has been working with area residents to create a new model for community development. It's a model, say Smith and others, that has as its foundation a belief that the community knows best what the community needs.

185

SERVICES BUILT AROUND SCHOOLS

At the heart of the Whitefoord Community Program are two schools: Whitefoord Elementary and Coan Middle, representing both literally and figuratively the future of the community. Every program, every cooperative project, says director Kenneth Lloyd, is designed with one central purpose in mind: to provide each and every child with whatever they need to succeed in school.

Students need more than an excellent academic program to succeed in school.

Given that mandate, it's not surprising that the Whitefoord Community Program has supported a wide range of educational programs and services for area youth. But its efforts don't stop there. Whitefoord residents know firsthand what the research has identified for years: that students need more than an excellent academic program to succeed in school. They need to be healthy, well fed, and surrounded by caring adults who are able to nurture their personal and academic growth. That's why, in addition to academic support programs like Head Start and Early Head Start, summer reading programs, and after-school tutorials, the Whitefoord Community Program includes two pediatric health clinics (one at each of the schools), job counseling, parenting classes, and much, much more.

"We take a holistic approach to education," explains director Lloyd, citing as an example the two health clinics on the elementary and middle school campuses. Thanks to these local services, families can obtain much-needed health care right in their own community. Parents don't need to take time off from work to get sick kids to the doctor. Regular check-ups mean students are less likely to get sick and miss days or weeks of school. And, thanks to the mental health services available at the middle school, students and their families are receiving much-needed (but previously unavailable) services to help them resolve conflicts, cope with stress, and treat mental illnesses.

A WHOLE-FAMILY APPROACH

Whether it's providing health care or computer training, virtually all of Whitefoord's programs have a family component. At the Family Learning Center, for example, the goal is to identify and provide programs that will assist the entire family—mothers and fathers, aunts and uncles, grandparents, and older siblings. To that end, the center offers GED classes, job training, and computer courses for adults, as well as a variety of after-school and summer enrichment programs for the eighteen hundred children in the one-square-mile community of Whitefoord.

The Whitefoord summer program offers community children a wide range of activities.

In Whitefoord, as in communities throughout the country, it is difficult for families to spend time together. Elementary school principal Patricia LaVant knows just how difficult it is. That's why she's particularly proud of a long-standing program at Whitefoord Elementary called Families and Students Together, or FAST. Once a week, parents and their children come together to share a meal, engage in an activity, and "just spend time talking to one another," says LaVant. Although the six-week program includes homework help for the students and parenting classes for the adults, the real value, LaVant points out, is the renewing of relationships between parents and children.

"It's about promoting quality conversations between parents and their children. It gives families a time to talk about their day—to see each other in a different light," says LaVant. "Hopefully," she adds, "it's building habits and relationships that will last a lifetime."

GIVING THE COMMUNITY WHAT IT WANTS

In keeping with its mission to be driven by the needs of the community, the Whitefoord Community Program has evolved over the years. First came the clinic at Whitefoord Elementary, next came child-care services and—most recently—a Computer Clubhouse for area youth, funded by the Intel Foundation. Over time, through hours and hours of discussion and a commitment to consensus-based decision making, the services have grown to meet the community's changing needs. One key component of this growth is the hiring of community residents themselves to serve as family advocates, teachers, counselors in the after-school program, and more.

> Instead of looking at the debts of a community, we believe in looking at its assets.

"Instead of looking at the debts of a community, we believe in looking at its assets," says Lloyd.

In Whitefoord, as in communities all over the country, it's the area residents who have the most to give—and the most to gain—by coming together to create a network of programs and services in support of education.

BEYOND WHITEFOORD: COMMUNITY SCHOOLS FLOURISH

Throughout the country, educators and parents, local government agencies, and community organizations are joining forces to create community schools. In communities as diverse as Long Beach, California, Wichita, Kansas, and New York City, these collaborations are providing students and families with the support and services necessary for children to thrive.

Although the specific composition and services vary, community schools share three key features: a strong academic component including tutoring, homework help, library services, and more; student and family support services, such as medical, dental, and mental heath clinics and on-site representatives from social service agencies; and academic and cultural enrichment activities for the entire community—from art and music classes for youth to computer and English as a Second Language classes for adults.

More important than any one program or service, though, is the role of a community school in bringing together families, educators, and students to lift up communities and give them hope.

- In the Washington Heights area of New York City, that hope has come in the form of nine community schools created through a partnership between the Children's Aid Society (CAS) and Community School District 6. Leadership teams composed of teachers, administrators, parents, and CAS staff have combined a rich set of academic and enrichment programs for youth with health care and immigrant services for families.

- In Long Beach, California, the YMCA Community School at Stevenson Elementary serves more than three hundred students and their families every week, providing everything from immigration services to science clubs, and from parent education classes to family reading nights. To ensure that after-school academic activities are aligned with the school curriculum, two teachers assist in the creation of the after-school academic activities and projects.

- Throughout the Tukwila School District in Washington, students and their families are benefiting from the development of community-school partnerships. The districtwide effort began with the introduction of after-school programs at the elementary schools and has expanded to include a range of services, including tutoring, parenting classes, and enrichment activities for the largely immigrant population.

- The doors are almost always open at Stanley Elementary School in Wichita, Kansas, where programs and activities are offered from 7 A.M. to midnight every day of the week. Volunteers from throughout the community work with school and community center staff to provide academic and enrichment activities for youth, family learning nights, literacy classes for adults, and more. The school site is also home to a district library and a senior center.

Jane Quinn, assistant executive director for community schools for the Children's Aid Society, describes the impact of community schools in this way: "We build an opportunity structure—opportunities for kids to expand their learning, for adults to be involved in learning and contributing to the school, for kids to contribute to their community, and for teachers to be involved with kids in different ways."

These new opportunities for youth, parents, and the entire community have paid off in a big way. Many community schools have reported gains on standardized tests, particularly in reading and mathematics. Parent involvement has skyrocketed, attendance has increased, and behavioral problems are reduced.

29

Community Technology Centers

A National Movement to Close the Digital Divide

MARK SARGENT

The movement started small, with a single center. In 1983, Antonia Stone opened "Playing To Win" in New York City's Harlem, creating the first center providing public access to personal computers in a low-income neighborhood. Long before the Internet, Stone, a math and science teacher, foresaw that computers would usher in exciting new opportunities for learning and that those without access risked being left behind. In those days, the center served more than five hundred people each week, including children whose local schools lacked enough computers, adults seeking new technology skills for the labor market, and people of all ages learning to use word processors, spreadsheets, and new ways to communicate.

CTCNET: NETWORKING CENTERS ON THE NET

Today, several technology generations later, the movement that Stone helped create is a central force in countering the continuing Digital Divide, that is, the gulf in access to technology tools and related learning opportunities imposed by socioeconomic status. "Playing To Win" developed into a small network of community access centers initially called "The Playing To Win Network," which later became the Community Technology Centers' Network (http://www.ctcnet.org). In 1995, after receiving a five-year grant from the National Science Foundation, CTCNet expanded first into a regional network of fifty-five affiliates and then into a national network of more than six hundred affiliates with more than four thousand locations, including settlement houses, after-school programs, church programs, adult literacy programs, and alternative schools.

The membership includes not only stand-alone technology access centers but large community organizations, including National Urban League affiliates, Boys and Girls Clubs, YMCAs, public libraries, and local cable access stations. CTCs in public libraries have been aided by major funding for hardware, software, and training from the Bill and Melinda Gates Foundation, which has linked more than seven thousand libraries in the United States and Canada to the Internet. In addition to schools, CTCs offer an important community-based environment in which young people, many from low-income and minority backgrounds, can use technology in creative learning experiences.

CTCs operated by these groups are helping to close the Digital Divide. The congressional Web-based Education Commission found that minority and low-income households were less likely to have computers and Internet access. An expanded definition of the "Divide" also highlights the lack of high-quality online content for those in underserved communities. A 2000 report from the Children's Partnership concluded, "It is as important to create useful content on the Internet—material and applications that serve the needs and interest of millions of low-income users and underserved Internet users—as it is to provide computers and Internet connections."

The following examples demonstrate how CTCs are providing young people in underserved communities with both technology access and the skills to become their own content creators.

PLUGGED IN GREENHOUSE

Teenagers come to the "Plugged In Greenhouse" in East Palo Alto, California, a low-income town on the edge of Silicon Valley, to learn about art and technology. But the larger mission of this after-school program is about creativity and innovation. "When you look around Silicon Valley," says the program's manager, Angela Booker, "the real technology pioneers are the ones who are innovative, who are creating new tools to solve problems. We use art as a springboard. We want to challenge kids to come up with their own ideas, to create things that come from their imagination, as opposed to consuming what others have created and posted on the Internet."

On a typical weekday afternoon, about twenty children, mostly African American, arrive at the Greenhouse, one of three programs hosted by Plugged In, one of the earliest community technology centers. The children participate in the program at least three afternoons a week, which helps ensure their projects will be productive. The "curriculum" consists of five units, each approximately ten weeks in duration, on topics such as people and places, business and entrepreneurship, and history and legend. For this latter unit, students in one group first researched the difference between history and legend, then decided to create their own legends, writing short stories and creating drawings to represent their characters. They performed their stories for one another and made a list of what they liked best about each story.

Up to this point, little technology was involved. The students then used the Greenhouse's digital video camera to create videos based on their stories, filming against the backdrops of sets and costumes they had also created. They also developed Web pages to introduce the characters they had created for their films. The results of their work, including a seven-minute film, are posted to the Plugged In Web site (http://www.pluggedin.org).

> Giving kids computer access will not on its own connect students to powerful ideas.

During another project on digital photography, students took digital cameras to different locations in the San Francisco Bay Area, including a redwood forest north of the Golden Gate Bridge. Students learned different photographic techniques and snapped images displayed at a gallery opening at the Palo Alto Art Center, at which they explained their techniques to visitors. These experiences, says Booker, give the students confidence in their own ability to create.

"When people talk about the Digital Divide, they usually advocate for greater access to technology," she explains. "But giving kids computer access will not on its own connect students to powerful ideas. But give a child the ability to take technology to a new place, then eventually, you'll bridge the gap."

SCIENCEQUEST

When a group of twelve- and thirteen-year-old students at the Castle Square Learning Center in south Boston began collecting water samples, they expected to find a difference in bacteria levels between river and pond samples. But they didn't expect to go on a field trip to the New England Aquarium and meet with Dr. Susan Goodridge, the scientist in charge of water quality for the aquarium's tanks. There, they worked behind the scenes in the wet lab and met Myrtle, the six hundred-pound turtle. They also didn't expect to learn that a small increase in ozone levels in water could spell the difference between life and death for Myrtle.

These twists and turns in real-life learning were part of ScienceQuest, an innovative after-school program offered through community technology centers in eastern Massachusetts. Funded by a three-year grant from the National Science Foundation, ScienceQuest organizes small teams of "investigators" at the centers to carry out hands-on investigations of scientific phenomena that interest them: static electricity on balloons, signs of spring outside the center door, or microorganisms in the Charles River. They work with "coaches"—specially trained volunteers from the community—and pursue their questions by getting outdoors—down to the river or off to the zoo.

The group of students collecting water samples from the Charles River, the Swan Pond in Boston Common, and tap water at the Castle Square Community Center compared the relative bacteria content by performing a variety of experiments. Happily, they discovered that their tap water was bacteria-free. They documented their project on a Web site named "Yucky Bacteria" hosted by ThinkQuest, the international youth Web site competition and a project partner (http://www.thinkquest.org).

The centerpiece of ScienceQuest's projects is a two-day training for the volunteer coaches covering three strands: working with students, including those with disabilities; working with science; and working with technology as a curriculum resource and as a tool to build Web sites. Coaches them-selves engage in a mini-project of their own. ScienceQuest also provides valuable con-nections to area science museums, zoos, and aquariums. The program is poised for expansion within Massachusetts and, ultimately, to CTCs around the country. "We've really touched a need," says project director Jennifer Dorsen. "After-school programs are really starved for projects that are low-cost and are straightforward to implement, *and* that engage kids productively in real science."

Students and adults participate in many academic and technology programs offered by the Baltimore Urban League.

PART 3

SKILLFUL EDUCATORS

The single most important factor in student success is teacher quality. Research has confirmed what seems like an obvious conclusion, but for years, school reform efforts have focused on other factors as the key to school improvement, such as improving textbooks, classifying students, or increasing testing.

To improve teacher quality and place more skillful educators in classrooms is not a simple job. Teaching is a complex enterprise, more complex than most nonteachers imagine. To be a skillful educator requires deep knowledge of the content to be taught and the ability to teach it to students who often have little background to draw upon. Teachers must be able to explain concepts in different ways, depending on the learning styles of their students. They also need to be part psychologist to deal with students' social and emotional issues, which often stand in the way of learning. And in this Digital Age, they also need to be fluent with technology and its many possibilities for enlivening the curriculum and documenting student progress.

No longer "sages on the stage" but not merely "guides on the side," skillful educators are still center stage. They are the hub of their students' learning and gather a growing number of learning resources, including books, computers, the Internet, and other adult experts. They bring the larger world to their students, which in turn expands their own knowledge of the subject.

Skillful educators also include principals, superintendents, and school board members—administrators who act as professional managers as well as instructional leaders. Their decisions control funding and other factors that enable teachers to do their best work. They, too, have complex and challenging positions, responsible not only for policies affecting teaching and learning but for physical plant, technology, personnel, legal and financial issues, community and media relations, and more. They also have needs for specific training to develop their capacities as educational leaders.

Skillful educators are lifelong learners, and they're raising our next generation of children to be lifelong learners as well.

Teacher Preparation

A quiet revolution is taking hold in colleges of education. Criticized for offering programs that are long on theory and short on practice, many schools of education have responded with new approaches to teacher education. These programs emphasize practical and extensive field experience as a key component of preparing new teachers. They prepare young college students to enter teaching as a first job and also prepare experienced professionals to make a career switch into teaching. Partnerships between universities and local schools are central to these model programs for beginning teachers.

The stories in this section feature the Curry School of Education at the University of Virginia, a career-switcher program at Colorado State University, and a university-school partnership in Cincinnati, Ohio, each demonstrating the kind of thoughtful and extensive support needed to prepare new teachers. An article from the University of Alabama shows how the handheld computer is proving to be a valuable device for student teachers and professors.

Following are some suggestions for how parents, educators, and policymakers can support better preparation of new teachers:

What parents can do:

- Support opportunities for new teachers to receive mentoring and classroom experience in local schools.

- Encourage local schools to establish partnerships for teacher preparation with colleges of education and other departments at local colleges and universities, along the model of a "professional development school."

- Encourage principals to look for extensive student teaching experience and expertise with technology in recruiting new teachers.

- Discuss teaching as a career option with your children and other young people, who may combine interests in other professions and disciplines with teaching.

What educators can do:

- Create local "professional development schools" in partnership with institutions responsible for teacher preparation.

- Develop programs to encourage professionals from other fields to enter teaching as a profession.

- Integrate technology in the preparation of new teachers as a tool for improving instruction and classroom management.

What policymakers can do:

- Ensure that field experience and mentoring from experienced teachers are strong components of teacher preparation in local districts and states.

- Support policies and funding so that new teachers enter the classroom able to integrate technology into their teaching.

- Ensure that schools of education are meeting national standards for accreditation and producing high-quality teacher candidates.

See accompanying DVD for related video clip.

30

The Right Stuff

Curry Graduates Leave College Prepared to Teach

SARA ARMSTRONG

Teacher-to-be Jessica Ozimek is nervous. The graduate student at the University of Virginia's Curry School of Education is about to see how a class of hard-to-impress high school sophomores reacts to a Web site she created to teach Renaissance art. And as if she weren't under enough pressure, her university adviser and supervising world history teacher will both be watching.

"I want to impress the kids, impress Ms. Howerton [history teacher Julie Howerton], and impress my [Curry] teacher," Ozimek says just before heading into the class. "And I'm really hoping I say and do the right thing."

She needn't have worried. The budding Renaissance scholars even offer compliments when Leonardo da Vinci's Mona Lisa suddenly pops onto their computer screens and when an interactive Web site about vanishing points proves to be fun and challenging.

And both Elaine Bartley, Ozimek's technology mentor from Curry, and Howerton are more than encouraging.

EARLY AND FREQUENT CLASSROOM EXPERIENCE

Ozimek is a beneficiary of Curry's belief that frequent practice in real classrooms is an essential requirement of high-quality teacher preparation. It is a sentiment she shares and one that led her to choose the education program at the handsome university Thomas Jefferson founded in Charlottesville.

> Frequent practice in real classrooms is an essential requirement of high-quality teacher preparation.

Curry overhauled its education program in the mid-1980s, anticipating two influential national reports that decried the inadequate preparation of teachers—who were leaving the profession in droves—and the schools that were supposed to be preparing them. Curry replaced its four-year teacher program with a five-year program. It eliminated the education undergraduate major, demanded subject matter mastery as well as knowledge of education theory, provided mentors through the first three years of teaching, instituted use of cutting-edge technology, and put heavy emphasis on real classroom experience.

Then-Dean Jim Cooper had so much confidence in the new program he offered a guarantee. Virginia superintendents who weren't 100 percent satisfied with Curry graduates could call upon a Curry faculty member to come to the school and get the new teacher up to speed. "We never had to go out to a single school," Cooper says proudly.

Curry's education program starts early despite the absence of an undergraduate education major. University of Virginia students considering teaching take a class called "Teaching as a Profession" as sophomores to help them understand the nature of classroom work with students. If they decide teaching is for them, they add education courses to their classload, which includes a major in an academic discipline. Sophomores observe in classrooms, juniors tutor students one on one, and seniors develop lessons for different grade levels and take those lessons to real classes. Fifth-year students spend the first semester in a classroom, shadowing and conferring with the classroom teacher, preparing and delivering lessons, and learning what it takes for a class to show academic progress. During the second semester, Curry students do a research project based on an issue that came up during their student teaching, and they prepare a portfolio that includes an online résumé.

Teacher candidate Jessica Ozimek engages students in a Web-based art history lesson she designed.

TREATING TEACHERS AS PROFESSIONALS

"How much time do lawyers get and how much time do medical doctors get to work under supervision?" asks Virginia Coffey, a veteran teacher who opens her Charlottesville kindergarten classroom to would-be teachers from Curry. Coffey, a graduate of Curry before its program was revamped, says she wishes she had more classroom experience while still in college. "It's a very sink-or-swim profession, so I think it's valuable that Curry has chosen to put them in earlier and give them more exposure over a period of time," she says.

Sophomore Alexa Kane has already learned about the importance of early exposure to a classroom. On one wintry day, the art history major watched as Coffey organized a class drawing and writing project based on a book the class had read. Kane sounded out letters with an earnest kindergartner. She read *The Gingerbread Man* to a group of enthralled students who eagerly joined in for the chorus: "Run, run, as fast as you can, you can't catch me, I'm the gingerbread man."

"Anytime you go into a classroom and just get a little more experience, you feel better the next time," Kane says. She adds that coming face to face with students in a classroom can be a sobering experience. Such "up in the clouds" goals as finding the uniqueness in each student get bumped against the realities of discipline, widely varying reading abilities, and looming standardized tests. "It's a lot harder than you think," she asserts.

> Coming face to face with students in a classroom can be a sobering experience.

A LEADER IN TECHNOLOGY

A decision was made at Curry, which has received numerous awards for its technology innovation and its Center for Technology and Teacher Education, not only to include emerging technology tools in instruction but also to lead in their development. Team-teaching with professors at colleges thousands of miles away, PowerPoint presentations by students and faculty, distance learning, electronic portfolios, and interactive collaborations and research are common elements of Curry programs.

"Our philosophy about using technology is that technology should be something that's not an add-on," states Joanne Herbert, assistant dean for admissions and student affairs at Curry and co-developer of CaseNEX, a multimedia case study program developed at Curry. "It should allow you to do things that you couldn't normally do in a classroom. So it's not lots of bells and whistles. It's trying to use technology in such a way that you help people learn more effectively."

CaseNEX allows student teachers to experience different classroom situations without actually being in the classroom. "We're talking about real life, and we're talking about it in real ways, and we're trying to understand what that is so that teachers will be better prepared to go out and teach," says Bob McNergney, Curry education professor and co-developer of CaseNEX.

For example, the largely white student body at Curry can get a clear idea of the issues involved in teaching at an inner-city school with large numbers of non-white or non–English-speaking students through a case study of New York City's Newcomers High School. They get an added perspective when they do an Internet video hookup—which they frequently do—with teacher candidates at the predominantly African American Hampton University on Chesapeake Bay.

Net-Frog, a highly acclaimed interactive frog dissection program that does away with formaldehyde, scalpels, and squeamishness, was developed by Curry faculty members, first on videodisc and then online.

Curry faculty members such as associate professor Randy Bell involve themselves and their students in experimental work with new technology tools, such as an inexpensive digital microscope that links to a computer and allows students to incorporate pictures taken through the microscope into their reports and presentations.

Curry graduate student Gerry Swan reviews student pictures taken with a digital microscope.

And the Technology Infusion Project pairs techno-savvy education students like Jessica Ozimek with less techno-savvy working teachers. Education students learn how to teach, and teachers learn how to use the Web and other technologies to enliven, deepen, and broaden their students' instruction.

"Yes! I really want to be a teacher."

In the end, the goal of Curry's comprehensive program, including technology, subject-matter mastery, classroom experience, and mentoring, is to produce excellent teachers who want to stay in the profession. Ozimek is evidence the program is clearly on the right track. "When it goes right, it's so rewarding," she beams. "I just drive back from the school and I'm like, 'Yes! I really want to be a teacher.'"

31

"Beyond Ready" to Teach

DIANE CURTIS

When many other first-year teachers were pulling out their hair and questioning why they went into education at all, Tonya Flannery and Tammy Seebohm were reveling in the daily joy of reaching children and watching the wide smiles and bright eyes that come with excitement about learning. Unlike many of their peers, whose inexperience forced them to concentrate on class management well into their first year, Seebohm and Flannery established a respectful classroom tone that allowed them to jump into productive academics right away.

The two young women credit their smooth start to the Cincinnati Initiative for Teacher Education (CITE), a collaboration among the University of Cincinnati (UC), the Cincinnati Public Schools, and the Cincinnati Federation of Teachers. A five-year program that results in dual bachelor's degrees in education and an academic discipline, CITE emphasizes classroom practice highlighted by a yearlong internship overseen by a mentor teacher, a university adviser, and a CITE coordinator at professional practice schools, also known as professional development schools. A related program has a Web site at http://www.uc.edu/certi.

> **If you don't get to practice, it isn't beneficial.**

During the internship, the UC student is in complete charge of the class for half the school day. The other half of the day may be taught by the veteran classroom teacher or by another intern. Many of the interns receive a partial first-year teacher's salary, which district and university officials credit with drawing more low-income students, for whom a year's unpaid internship might have been an impassable barrier. The internships are often in hard-to-staff inner-city schools. Many of the students end up dedicated to urban education, taking their first teaching jobs in some of Cincinnati's toughest neighborhoods.

THE ANSWERS ARE NOT IN THE TEXTBOOK

"You can't just read about it in a textbook," says Flannery, who began her third year of elementary school teaching in Cincinnati's inner city in 2001. "If you don't get to practice, it isn't beneficial." "The experience I had was just unbelievable," agrees Seebohm, a fourth-grade teacher in Hamilton, Ohio. "When I went into my own classroom, I was beyond ready."

UC taught her both the subject matter and how to teach it, Seebohm says. The internship taught her how to use that knowledge and how to create, from day one, a classroom culture that promoted learning. From her observations and intern experience, Seebohm set the tone by laying out classroom rules honed in her internship year. Flannery took a slightly different approach, using a program called "The Responsive Classroom" to teach respect and caring for one another and to "create a little family."

THE BEST PREPARATION FOR TEACHING

"Though you prepare for teaching by taking courses, the best preparation is teaching itself," former U.S. Secretary of Education Richard Riley has said in praising the CITE program. "To learn with the support of master teachers is absolutely critical, and I think teaching colleges are beginning to realize this."

Prospective teachers who enroll at UC begin education courses in their second year, including a short K–12 field experience, with additional education courses in their third year. In their fourth year, they become what are called "teaching associates." One day each week, they help teach one class throughout the school year. In the fifth year, they complete the internship, supplemented with courses allowing them to further analyze and refine their classroom work.

They also pick up valuable tips, such as accepting silence as a way to allow a student to formulate an answer or comment, keeping cereal or crackers on hand for kids who come to class hungry, and speaking more softly to calm a class rather than shouting to be heard over the uproar. The interns also complete a portfolio that reflects their year's work.

The interns are considered real teachers, with all responsibilities that the title implies— from setting up the classroom in the fall and writing lesson plans to holding parent conferences, overseeing extracurricular activities, and serving on faculty committees.

Damon Davis, a first-year teacher who was hired by a Cincinnati school after completing his internship there last year, says that being considered a professional enhanced his experience. "It really gives you some ownership of the classroom. Kids see you not as a student teacher—someone who is just there for a short period of time—but as your teacher who's there every day. And ownership is an important part of class management."

Ownership is an

important part of

class management.

NEW TEACHERS HIT THE GROUND RUNNING

Flannery says second-year teacher friends who experienced the limited but typical ten weeks of student teaching at other colleges "still say they don't know what to do" whether setting up rules for pencil sharpening or going to the bathroom or attempting to elicit thoughtful student answers in class. In contrast, UC graduates are asked by their principals to contribute teaching ideas to other teachers and to take on leadership roles. As Seebohm puts it, "There was definitely a difference in the confidence level."

Veteran teacher Sandra Luebbe points out that interns aren't alone in benefiting from the program. A mentor at an inner-city school for eight years, Luebbe says the interaction with students and professors, as well as participation in professional practice school seminars and workshops, helped her keep abreast of new education reforms, such as cooperative learning and *constructivist*—that is, project—learning. She found her role of adviser to be professionally satisfying, allowing her to influence not just her own class but others as well.

EARNED CONFIDENCE FROM CONSTANT MENTORING

Terress Reid, who went through the CITE program after earning an undergraduate degree in mental health from Northern Kentucky University, says mentoring from both her UC adviser and a mentor teacher gave her the confidence to feel comfortable about taking over her own class this fall.

When Reid was an intern, UC associate professor Ronald Sterling showed up in her class every Wednesday to check on how things were going and answer her questions. Every day before school, she would go over her lesson plan with her classroom mentor. And every day after school, they would talk about what had worked, what hadn't, and how her teaching and class management style could be improved. Reid learned that simple changes, such as altering the seating arrangement, could make a huge difference in classroom behavior.

MATE interns work with the school technology coordinator as part of their teacher preparation.

"I don't see how you could teach without that experience," Reid recalls. "It's kind of like being a doctor and not having ever operated on anybody."

Related Web site: www.uc.edu/certi

A PLACE TO DISCOVER THE TEACHER WITHIN

VIRGINIA WATKINS AND CECELIA WAMBACH

What happens when you bring a cohort of thirty teacher education students into an urban school? You sow the seeds of powerful and lasting change—for both the university teacher education program and the school—in this case, John Muir Elementary School in San Francisco, California.

The Muir Alternative Teacher Education Program (MATE) is the result of a collaboration between San Francisco State University and the San Francisco Unified School District. Its mission is to create a new model for elementary school teaching and a new model for teacher preparation.

At the heart of this seven-year-old program is the concept that each of us—administrators, teachers, and students—is unique and has wisdom to share with others. In mentoring one another, we have created a nurturing, caring, learning community where children are thriving educationally, emotionally, and socially, and teacher interns are learning how to teach.

Planting Seeds

Interns arrive at Muir during August while teachers are setting up their classrooms. They visit from class to class and talk with teachers about their curricula, teaching

Virginia Watkins and Cecelia Wambach started the MATE program and served as co-principals at John Muir Elementary School for seven years. When Dr. Wambach returned to San Francisco State University (SFSU) full-time in 2001, Ms. Watkins became sole principal. SFSU lecturer Pat Chandler became director of the MATE program at the school site, thus retaining the true partnership between Muir and the University in producing capable teachers.

styles, types of classroom activities, summer vacation, and other matters of the heart. After spending time with the teachers, interns select which grade levels they want to teach for the upcoming year: K–1, 2–3, or 4–5.

After two days of classroom visits, the interns meet with the entire teaching staff to share personal stories. After getting to know the students, each teacher then selects two candidates who seem likely to work well as interns in class.

Developing Mutual Respect

Keeping in mind the preferences of both the interns and the teachers, we create pairings that represent as diverse a group as possible for our children. In forming mentoring partnerships, we consider issues such as gender, race, and special interests. We see this process as planting the seeds of a long-lasting professional relationship.

Instead of taking classes at the university and spending just one semester as a student teacher, MATE interns teach and take their courses at this inner-city elementary school. We have found that our immersion approach to teacher education works best for interns who want the rigorous experience of participating in solutions for urban education.

University Courses in the Classroom

Our interns become our curriculum assistants and idea partners, providing mini-group instruction in our classrooms and helping us devise better ways to educate our students. They provide one-on-one instruction and interventions to students whenever special help is needed. They are storytellers, game teachers, and writing assistants.

Sometimes they become the teachers while the teacher assists. And when they are comfortable doing so, they serve as substitutes when teachers are out of the class-room for workshops or other professional-development experiences.

Turning the Tables

As interns begin to open up and take risks in their teaching, the entire classroom community wakes up to what learning is all about. For our interns, this is what it means to "discover the teacher within."

In this place of self-discovery, children begin taking risks with their own thinking and begin working in deeper ways. They become inquisitive learners, relishing time for reading, participating eagerly in projects, proudly performing their latest drama, and showing off their first published novel in second grade!

Mentorship relationships between interns and mentor teachers are one facet of our supportive school community. School district and university personnel mentor each other and the teachers. The entire community mentors the children. Our school is the creation of our entire community.

 **See accompanying DVD for related video clip.**

32

Making the Switch to Teaching

ROBERTA   FURGER

From the time he was just a young kid, Denny Heyrman knew he was born to teach. It just took him a little longer than most people to realize his life dream.

At fifty-one—an age when many men and women are beginning to think about retirement—Heyrman has embarked on a new profession as a high school teacher. It's the burly Wisconsin native's third career—he worked as a butcher for thirty years and as a geologist for four—but after just a few minutes of conversation, you know that he's found a home teaching earth science at Loveland High School in Loveland, Colorado.

Heyrman is one of thousands of midcareer professionals throughout the United States stepping up to help fill the much talked-about teacher shortage. But unlike many who come to teaching through nontraditional routes, he wasn't thrown into the classroom after just a few short weeks of "boot camp" or handed an emergency credential and a class roster. Instead, Heyrman began his first teaching assignment with classroom experience in five different school settings and many hours of instruction in everything from technology integration to teaching students with diverse needs and abilities. He's the product of Colorado State University's Project Promise, an innovative, one-year graduate-level program specifically designed for men and women making a midcareer switch to teaching.

A COMMUNITY OF LEARNERS

From the time codirectors Barbara McWhorter and Angie Paccione start reviewing the roughly two hundred applications they receive each year until students and faculty say their farewells at graduation, everything about Project Promise hinges on the development of a close, supportive group—or in academese, a cohort. The new student teachers bring a wide range of professional and life experience into their classrooms: naturalists and environmental educators, mechanical and chemical engineers, lawyers and social workers, business managers, and even a toy designer, a carpenter, and a professor of Chinese literature.

The instructors model the teaching styles they want their students to employ.

The first few weeks of the program are devoted to building trust and respect among the roughly twenty students who comprise each Project Promise class and their two instructors, McWhorter and Paccione. They complete a ropes course, share personal stories, and even play an old-fashioned game of Red Rover.

During those early weeks, the instructors begin modeling the teaching styles they want their students to employ. In a lesson on developing respect and trust in a classroom, for example, McWhorter and Paccione demonstrate an activity they call "The

People Bag," during which they introduce themselves by sharing personal items. A "people bag" can be anything from a suitcase (for someone who loves to travel) to a kayak, which is what one river lover used to carry his most treasured possessions to class. One by one, teachers and students share their bags, a technique that many long-time graduates continue to use with their new students at the beginning of the school year.

"They're not just teaching us the material we need for certification," says Heyrman. "They're getting up and demonstrating how to get involved with the kids. They're setting the example they want us to follow."

Project Promise students discuss their recent classroom experiences.

COMBINING THEORY AND PRACTICE

After those early weeks of team building, students spend a week at a local public school, where they observe how a teacher prepares a classroom and begins to shape a group of twenty or thirty students into a community of learners. "Theory and practice go hand in hand," explains co-director Paccione. "We give students a chunk of theory, then we let them practice it. We bring them back for some more theory, then they go out and practice again."

The mixing of theory and practice applies to the teaching of technology as well. Early on in the program, students participate in what Paccione describes as a technology boot camp, where everyone is brought up to speed on application basics: sending and receiving e-mail, creating various spreadsheet and word processing documents, and using desktop presentation software tools. From there, students begin using these tools to create lessons they'll be using throughout their student teaching experiences.

Because students enter Project Promise with at least a bachelor's degree and often work experience in the subject area they will be teaching, McWhorter and Paccione focus their instruction on helping students transform their subject-area specialty into thoughtful, engaging lesson plans. Whether creating a review game or developing cooperative learning activities, students are expected to apply the tools and strategies they've learned to their specific subject areas. For more focused instruction, students are also required to take a subject-specific teaching methods course through the CSU College of Education.

The Project Promise program includes multiple experiences for its teacher candidates.

"I had the background in geology," says Heyrman. "Through Project Promise I learned how to prepare lesson plans, how to engage kids, and I got hours and hours of hands-on teaching experience."

STUDENT-CENTERED INSTRUCTION

A unique three-week Diversity Institute prepares students for the complexities of teaching children of different genders, cultures, socioeconomic backgrounds, and learning abilities. Throughout the Institute, students are encouraged to examine their own teaching practices and to spend time understanding "and hopefully overcoming" their personal biases, says McWhorter. They also spend a week as a student teacher in an urban high school in Denver, where they have the opportunity to again put theory into practice.

Throughout the program, students benefit from the support and advice of peers, supervising teachers, and their Project Promise instructors. During their final nine-week student teaching experience in area high schools, for example, students meet with their cooperating teacher (in whose class they are student teaching) at least twice a week and discuss everything from lesson planning and delivery to interaction with students. Issues discussed are documented in a binder that McWhorter and Paccione refer to during their weekly visits to their students' classrooms. They also benefit from regular, though less formal, feedback from classmates who are student teaching at the same school.

Besides the feedback from peers and supervisors, students are encouraged to become their own critics and coaches. From their first day in the program, students keep a journal in which they reflect daily on what they've learned, lessons they've taught, and concerns that keep them up at night. Although McWhorter and Paccione respond to the journal entries, the real value, say students and instructors, is in the self-reflection that goes along with the journal writing.

Videotaping plays a similar role for the would-be teachers. Much as athletes review their performance after a big game, students are routinely videotaped as they "practice" giving lessons to their Project Promise classmates and teach courses at local middle and high schools. "It's not often that teachers articulate and observe what we do," says McWhorter. "We want each experience to be meaningful, to be preparation for the next step," she adds. "Reflective practice helps them to do that."

THE FIRST-YEAR SAFETY NET

Even the best teacher education programs cannot fully prepare a new teacher for the daily highs and lows of running a classroom for the first time, as evidenced by the high dropout rate among first-year teachers. That's why Project Promise staff continue to support their students through formal and informal mentoring even after they've graduated from the program. "They ask our feedback on lesson plans and resources and invite us to come and observe their classes," says McWhorter, who with Paccione makes the rounds to local schools to check in with graduates, offering advice and encouragement.

And just as students help one another get through the program, they provide both practical and emotional support to one another as graduates. "I really feel a kinship with every other Project Promise graduate," says Heyrman. "We have a shared experience that makes us close, even among graduates from different years."

Related Web site: http://promise.colostate.edu/

Versatile Handheld Computers Aid Mobile Student Teachers

ANNA C. MCFADDEN, BARRIE JO PRICE, AND GEORGE E. MARSH II

Students preparing to be teachers can make their professional lives run more smoothly—as well as get a head start on learning how to engage students—with a very compact, easy-to-use electronic organizer known as a personal digital assistant (PDA).

Wearing a PDA in a clip case attached at the waist or on a tether around the neck, teachers can electronically jot down their observations about individual students as they walk around a classroom. They can input grades and coordinate schedules with colleagues who have PDAs. They can read papers on the run and share lesson plans while passing each other in school corridors.

Susan Patterson, doctoral student at the University of Alabama, Beverly Ray, Ph.D., Idaho State University, and teachers in the Tuscaloosa, Alabama, City School System also contributed to this article.

As faculty working with student teachers at the University of Alabama, we use our PDAs to manage student appointments and class grades. Our students beam their word processing assignments to us—and we beam them back.

The PDA (with product names such as Palm, Handspring Visor, or Rim Blackberry) generally includes a name and address database, to-do list, and notetaker. PDAs typically allow people to use a pen to tap selections on menus and to enter printed characters, and some models also include a small onscreen keyboard operated by pen taps. Their prices range from just over $100 to $500.

The following sections describe applications especially useful to student teachers.

INTERNET ACCESS AND E-MAIL: DATA CHARTING

To begin a unit on charting data and learning to display various types of data in different formats, the classroom teacher has brought in the local newspaper for the students to find weather-related data to chart. The student teacher can download Web pages to his PDA and can display the Weather Channel.com, so that students have access to a wider range of data. Students can see the data on the PDA and use it at a work center without Internet access, since the number of connections in the classroom is limited.

We use our PDAs to manage student appointments and class grades.

INTERNET ACCESS AND E-MAIL: SHARING LESSON PLANS

Teachers and student teachers can beam lesson plans among themselves as they pass in the hallway and comment on them while on recess duty. Returning from the playground, she can pause at her teammate's door to beam her revisions to the teammate prior to their planning meeting after school.

If the school has an internal computer network, the teachers can *hot-sync*—that is, instantly transmit lesson planning documents to their laptops or desktops—and then merge them into one document over the school's network and produce a final collective document. The principal or lead teacher can print the document for meetings later that day. The final document can be sent to each teacher via e-mail or posted on the school's server. Teachers can walk out of the building with a copy of the final plans on the PDA. It beats carrying around all that paper!

INTERNET ACCESS AND E-MAIL: READING FOR PROFESSIONAL DEVELOPMENT

For teachers and student teachers, time to peruse Web pages may be very limited, not by interest or even by time, but by time online. Educators with PDAs can catch up on professional reading while riding a commuter train or waiting at soccer meets and piano lessons. For instance, Web sites can be downloaded for review on a PDA without an Internet connection.

DOCUMENT SHARING AND PORTABILITY: READING AND GRADING PAPERS

A student teacher is doing a unit on bicycle safety in a sixth-grade classroom for a course in the teacher training program. The unit requires students to review a set of Internet links on bicycle safety and do independent research on the nature of injuries, types of equipment, and "rules of the road." The students are to prepare individual essays using word processing and, working in teams, to collaboratively design and develop a Web page as a resource on bicycle safety.

The sixth graders send their essays to the student teacher attached to e-mail messages. The teacher then syncs each student's document from her desktop computer to the PDA, making it possible to work anywhere—carpool, student union, or university hallway—while waiting for class to begin. Using a feature to track changes in the document, the student teacher or other student reviewers can provide feedback to the writer within the document.

When grading is completed, the student teacher can return the graded work to the students by e-mail or in a printed version. And when the PDA has special software designed for teachers to input grading, attendance, and contact data, grades and other information can be easily retained and then moved to a desktop.

CLASSROOM AND DATA MANAGEMENT: ASSIGNING STUDENT WORK GROUPS

A student teacher working in a ninth-grade history class has been asked to help the classroom teacher arrange work groups for an assignment on the polling process. He observes students working in groups and, using the PDA that dangles from his neck, he posts short observations for later review. He asks students some carefully chosen questions based on grouping research and records their answers in a word processing document on his PDA. Later, he sits at the side of the room, using his PDA and his folding keyboard, and records specific classroom comments and events.

The PDA makes it possible to work anywhere.

He prepares a word-processing document on his desktop computer for the teacher and downloads the final draft onto his PDA. The next day he reads it one more time on his way to school and makes corrections. At school, he beams his final version to the history teacher's PDA for the teacher to review over the weekend. On Monday, they collectively consider how to structure the work groups for the upcoming polling project.

PRODUCTIVITY: SETTING UP A TEAM PLANNING MEETING

Six student teachers are discussing the need to make exploration kits for third graders for a health unit. Each needs to buy certain food items and bring them to a meeting to be assembled into kits for student teams. The challenge is to find a time when the group can meet, allowing enough time to pick up the items at the grocery store.

Someone offers to be the team leader and set up the meeting. The others put their avail-

able times in their calendars and, while they are still in the meeting room, beam their week's schedule to the team leader. Looking at the composite week's calendar, the team leader can tell when a common meeting time is available and can beam it back to all members if they are all still together, or send them the meeting time via e-mail if they've gone on to other activities.

Students use handhelds for data collection and research.

Ongoing Professional Development

It used to be that new teachers were assigned to their classrooms and expected to close the door and teach based on what they had learned in their college courses. Now educators, like other professionals, require a commitment to lifelong learning and development to stay current with knowledge in their fields. And like other professionals, teachers learn best from others who face the same challenges they do—namely, other teachers.

Strong professional development programs for teachers involve teachers learning from other teachers, through close examination of actual student work. Such programs rely on schools and districts to provide ample time for this type of professional exchange.

The first three years of teaching are critical ones for learning the art of teaching when given full responsibility for an entire class of students. Pairing new teachers with experienced mentor teachers is critical to their success and retention in the teaching profession. The Santa Cruz New Teacher Project described here is a national model for supporting novice teachers.

Mentoring is also valuable in equipping teachers with technology skills, as implemented at the University of Texas at El Paso. One key set of technology skills teachers will need to convey to students is "information literacy." Kathy Schrock, a school media librarian, describes this set of skills and exemplifies the professional development role that many media librarians provide for their teachers. TAPPED IN—an online space for collaborative work to support the continued learning of teachers—is also profiled.

Here are several action steps for parents, educators, and policymakers to support the continuing development of teachers:

What parents can do:

- With your PTA or school site council, advocate for ongoing professional development opportunities for teachers, during the school year and in the summer.

- Discuss with teachers the types of professional development they have found most valuable.

- Provide teachers and principals with Web sites and other online resources offering professional development for teachers through model curricula and exchanges with other teachers.

What educators can do:

- Take advantage of professional development opportunities individually and with others in your school and district. These can include both in-person and online workshops and courses. Some of these continue as online support groups and learning communities.

- Communicate useful new ideas and practices from these workshops and courses to faculty in your school and district.

- Advocate for school policies to make more time available for educators to engage in professional development.

What policymakers can do:

- Create policies that encourage a "culture of learning" for teachers, including funding, time, and opportunities for meaningful professional development.

- Work with businesses, universities, and community-based organizations such as science centers and museums to develop professional development opportunities for teachers.

- Consider how technology can support the continuing learning needs of teachers and other educators in districts and states.

Supporting New Teachers During Their First Years in Teaching

ELLEN MOIR

In the last decade, we've come to understand that novices entering teaching, like those entering any profession, need an "induction phase"—a developmental process in which new teachers receive ongoing support, opportunities for professional growth, and a means of receiving continual feedback during the first few years.

THE STATUS QUO IS NOT WORKING

The traditional method of launching a teacher's career rests on the myth that teacher credential program graduates are prepared to teach unassisted in a classroom. Historically, we treat new teachers the same as we do veteran teachers. That means we give them a key to their room and say, "Here you go, and good luck."

That system hasn't worked. Up to 50 percent of unsupported new teachers leave the profession within five years, at a time when the country is in desperate need of qualified new teachers. According to the U.S. Department of Education, 2 million new teachers must be hired by 2010 due to class size reduction, a demographic bulge of teachers approaching retirement, and a scandalously high attrition rate among new teachers.

Unsupported new teachers who leave the profession within five years: up to 50 percent.

Regardless of the quality of their preparation, teachers in their first year face an overwhelming number of concerns, such as setting up a new classroom, developing curricula for a new group of students with wide ranges of abilities, grading papers, learning to talk with parents, and dealing with an endless cascade of paperwork and other minutiae. Often, due to the nature of day-to-day classroom teaching, these issues must be dealt with quickly and, in the traditional system, without anyone to turn to for advice. New teachers working in isolation navigate a slow and painful learning curve.

Using this trial-by-fire method exacts a high price on new teachers, their students, and the entire school community. Faced with a multitude of problems and a lack of support, new teachers quickly become disillusioned, and many leave the profession.

We simply can't afford to continue with the status quo.

A CATALYST FOR CHANGE: THE SANTA CRUZ NEW TEACHER PROJECT

A remedy for a system that discourages new teachers has been well documented at the Santa Cruz New Teacher Project. With the appropriate assistance, counsel, and instruction, fledging teachers can usually maintain their enthusiasm for being in the classroom.

Beginning teachers in the Santa Cruz New Teacher Project who have had the continuous support of a talented mentor have greater job satisfaction and are much more likely to continue teaching. For example, 94 percent of the teachers who began our program in 1992–93 are still in the profession.

Our experience in working with more than four thousand beginning teachers shows that performance in the classroom is greatly accelerated when teachers receive ongoing support. In our surveys with principals, they often report that first-year teachers from our program perform like third-year teachers. Having the support of a mentor helps new teachers develop and reflect on classroom strategies, set up long- and short-term curriculum plans, and set the kind of learning environment they would like in their classrooms. This type of dedicated support enhances teacher development and satisfaction.

> **Santa Cruz New Teacher Project retention rate: 94 percent of the 1992–93 cohort.**

In addition to curriculum development and teaching support, mentors offer emotional support at a time when a teacher is a beginner in a new profession. When someone else is there to say, "When back-to-school night comes in two weeks, these are the kinds of questions parents will be asking," new teachers get a boost in confidence and a jump on what is to be expected.

DRAWING ON VETERANS' EXPERTISE

The most significant component of any induction program is the quality of the experienced teacher who works with the new teacher. Like teaching, mentoring new teachers effectively is an ongoing learning process. Building these teachers' skills as leaders is something we take seriously. In the Santa Cruz New Teacher Project, we provide weekly professional development meetings where mentors—known as advisers—discuss progress and concerns about their mentoring and learn effective strategies to move beginning teacher practice forward.

In our model, we release exemplary teachers for two or more years to work with a caseload of fourteen beginning teachers, which offers a new role for expert teachers. To give this cadre of mentor teachers the set of skills necessary to be successful, we offer instruction not only about classroom practice but also about group facilitation, conflict resolution, presentation skills, running effective meetings, and collecting and analyzing student work against content standards. The teachers also learn how to use the data—which may include test scores, report cards, student work, and other formative assessments—to guide classroom instruction.

LEARNING TO TEACH NEW TEACHERS

The new teacher advisers are carefully matched with beginning teachers according to grade level and subject matter. They meet with new teachers weekly in their classrooms to observe, coach, and offer emotional support. They help with planning, suggest classroom management strategies, teach demonstration lessons, assist with assessment, and facilitate communication with principals. A mentor's support can be contextualized: "When I was in your classroom, I was wondering about your grouping strategy. What outcomes did you want for student learning? What did you notice happening?" The mentor also has a vision for what an excellent classroom should look like and might ask, "Is there equity of participation? Do all students have access to the curriculum?" Advisers work to build strong, trusting relationships, which become fundamental to the success of all support and assessment strategies. Online tools such as e-mail and Web sites provide additional opportunities for mentors and new teachers to share questions and concerns and extend their relationship beyond face-to-face interactions.

Mentoring a new teacher helps the veteran learn and grow as never before. Veteran teachers have a chance to step out of their classrooms and observe new teachers in many different teaching situations. They broaden their perspective of effective teaching and learn to articulate the expertise they have developed over their career. They also have a chance to reflect on their own practices. When they return to their districts and continue teaching, they return with a new set of skills and knowledge. These teachers emerge as leaders in their district and community.

> Advisers work to build strong, trusting relationships— fundamental to the success of all support and assessment strategies.

COLLABORATIVE LEARNING CULTURES

Supporting new teachers represents one of the most significant reform efforts that has ever landed in our public schools. By addressing the needs of new teachers, we often remove many of the barriers that traditionally keep teachers isolated. Even in schools where only a single teacher receives support, the message is sent that teaching and ongoing teacher learning matter. Teachers see that collaboration and teacher-to-teacher support is important.

Where large numbers of new teachers receive support, we see entire schools engaged in continuous conversations about teaching and student learning. In these learning communities, teachers come together to collect and analyze student work, which then informs curriculum development and instructional practices. These processes promote accountability and improve student achievement schoolwide. Ongoing support of all teachers becomes a regular part of the daily routines of the classroom and the school.

ADVANCING THE TEACHING PROFESSION

Supporting new teachers represents a major shift in thinking about the teaching pro-

fession. Addressing the skills and knowledge necessary to help new teachers be successful raises new questions about how to design learning communities in schools where students, veteran teachers, and administrators can be successful. This work requires new ways of thinking about teaching and learning. It requires new norms and practices of professionalism, career-long learning, and inquiry into the practice of teaching.

The next ten years are crucial for the teaching profession. The reality is that learning to teach is a lifelong process, and it takes time. We need to not only recruit great teachers but give them the kind of ongoing, steady support and development that will sustain them over their career. Money, time, and energy must be focused on creating a profession in which teachers, both novice and veteran, can thrive. Only then will our students reap the benefits.

Related Web site: www.newteachercenter.org

Teachers Helping Teachers

The Path to School Improvement

JORGE DESCAMPS

Every Monday morning at 8 o'clock, Gloria Contreras joins her team of third-grade teachers at H.D. Hilley Elementary School to discuss strategies for integrating technology with classroom activities. Experienced and beginning teachers alike bring their questions to the meeting:

> How do I find the time to use Hyperstudio with my science activities?
>
> How do I evaluate technology-based lessons?
>
> How can I increase the memory in my computer to run my software?

As a technology mentor teacher, Gloria listens to these questions and shares her ideas with her colleagues. Both Gloria and her mentees benefit from the experience: Teachers learn how technology can transform traditional instruction, and Gloria deepens her practice by reflecting on her own teaching with technology.

Gloria is part of an innovative mentoring program resulting from a partnership between the University of Texas at El Paso (UTEP) and area public schools. Two U.S. Department of Education Technology Innovation Challenge Grants have enabled 350 teachers to enroll in a UTEP master's program integrating educational technology and teaching. The centerpiece of the program is a mentoring class designed to enhance the technology and leadership skills of teachers as they mentor other teachers. By sponsoring the use of mentoring to transform classroom teaching, this grant has been one of the primary forces driving the school technology reform agenda in El Paso. As graduates such as Gloria mentor at least three other teachers at their schools, an estimated one thousand teachers will benefit from the program by the end of the grant period in 2003.

Gloria Contreras assists teachers in developing evaluation standards and rubrics for technology-based projects.

FROM THEORY TO PRACTICE

Why a separate course on mentoring? Because the theory taught at many universities does not necessarily translate into classroom practice. During the course, Gloria practiced her mentoring skills with a cohort of five teachers. "We developed skills for effective interpersonal communication, such as being a good listener and providing meaningful support and guidance to our colleagues. Not only did we learn the theory, we learned how to support each other," she says.

For example, using their skills from the course, the cohort developed an integrated unit on air pollution—a topic of great concern in El Paso, a metropolitan area of 700,000 sitting on the Rio Grande. Gloria and her colleagues discussed the role of technology, conducted research, collaboratively wrote the lessons, and chose appropriate graphics and software for the topic. Continually reflecting on the lesson objectives, members of the group mentored each other every step of the way. At the start of the course, some cohort members were strong writers; others were more technically savvy or had better research skills. Over time, however, all members were able to improve upon all these skills; each teacher learned to give and receive support in a nonthreatening atmosphere.

As Gloria says of the experience, "In order for us to learn, we had to learn together."

Underlying the UTEP course is the assumption that mentoring involves more than just teaching others how to use technology. It also involves guiding class members as they discover new ways to use technology most effectively and working to resolve the challenges they encounter while helping other teachers use technology. Gloria practiced how to be a mentor through simulation and role-playing. The instructor divided the class into small groups. Half of the participants played the role of mentors and the other half played the role of mentees, reenacting situations they experienced at their schools. Group discussions followed these dramatizations.

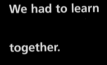

We had to learn together.

BECOMING A LEARNING ORGANIZATION

The mentoring course gives teachers a clinical setting in which to examine and share their teaching practices with the instructor and cohort members. The mentoring relationships developed in the course help break down walls that in the past have isolated teachers, allowing colleagues to become members of a team. By continuously reflecting on their practice, the mentors experience their own professional growth at the university and at their schools, which helps each school become a "learning organization" where participants support each other as they integrate technology into curricula.

Back at her school, Gloria took "baby steps" to help other teachers learn to use technology. "I thought, there's no way I could mentor other teachers, motivate them, or get them enthused—it's just going to be too much work. Then I realized that if I could get one teacher interested, I could get others interested. So I visited first-grade teacher Maria Aguilera and saw her students' beautifully written stories hanging on the wall. I asked Maria if I could borrow the students' work and put the stories into Hyperstudio. Maria and her students saw how the technology transformed their work, making it look professional with added sound and graphics features. As Maria witnessed her students' enthusiasm, she decided to accept the challenge herself and worked with me to learn how to implement technology in her classroom. As a mentor, I had my first mentee."

EXCHANGING IDEAS

During Gloria's initial meetings at her school, she asked teachers what areas of technology use they were most interested in. She then used her own students' writings to highlight how technology tools support learning. "Teachers at my school would say, 'I like what you are doing, but how do I get my students started using technology?' This is exactly how the mentoring course supported me. I demonstrated an idea to make the lesson more concrete for our teachers, and they learned valuable skills, such as using a scanner and converting files using multimedia tools. Our first step as a group was to develop a five-point rubric for assessing technology-based lessons. These rubrics help students understand what is expected of them by defining what kind of work earns five points, four points, and so on. For me, the rubrics provide a means for assessing the students' projects. These rubrics are now posted in each room."

A mentor helps reduce the anxiety of new learners by adjusting learning tasks to fit their proficiency level. Without one-on-one mentoring, many teachers are afraid to use technology in

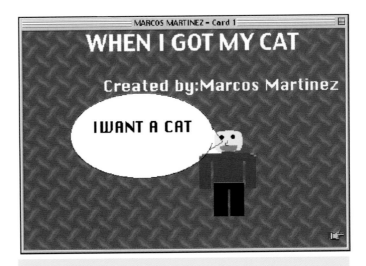

First graders create multimedia stories that include original art work, graphics, and sound.

their classrooms. Leslie Chavez, one of Gloria's mentees, explains, "I had three computers in my classroom and never knew what to do with them. With a mentor's help, I've been able to realize what is possible. We've expanded our Writer's Workshop by having students create and publish their own stories using computers. Gloria is here when the questions come up, and the ongoing day-to-day contact makes the difference. I was afraid to use technology because it's hard to show students something I don't know. Now I feel comfortable letting students work through problems that may arise with the technology. I was afraid they would learn it 'wrong,' and now I know that's not true. The students often help me."

The experiences of Gloria, Maria, and Leslie are not unique. Graduates of the UTEP program are taking the skills they learn back into their classrooms. They are mentoring colleagues in their schools and are more involved in campus technology planning activities. They report that their students are working more cooperatively, are learning more, and are more willing to try new things. Through its innovative use of mentoring, the UTEP program is providing teachers with the skills to transform their schools into twenty-first-century learning institutions.

Information Literacy

KATHY SCHROCK

Now more than ever, students' ability to analyze what they see and hear—in all media—is vital. With the proliferation of information sources on the Internet, and in television, radio, and print, the skills of "information literacy" can help students understand what they are being told, how to assess it for veracity, and how to use what they've found.

OLD CONCEPTS, NEW MEDIA

The concepts underlying information literacy are not new. The idea that students must first decide what type of information they need, figure out where to find the information, consider how to find the information, and then determine if the information meets their needs, has always been the basis of the traditional research cycle. It used to be easy—students used an encyclopedia or other print reference sources to acquire a knowledge base about their topic, a periodical guide to locate relevant magazine and journal articles, and books to gather in-depth information. Now, however, the sources available to gather information have exploded to include online material such as Web sites, e-zines, and direct communication with experts.

The underlying essentials of gathering information have not changed, either. Students still need to figure out what information they are looking for, use a source to acquire knowledge about a topic, search and evaluate the information they find, and compare it to what they already know about the topic to see if it meets their needs. They need to know both the old methods and sources and the new ones and to be able to assess the value of a greater variety of materials.

START WITH WHAT YOU KNOW

In helping teachers and parents in my district, Nauset Public Schools on Cape Cod, become familiar with the process of information literacy using the Internet, I often start with a topic they know something about. Having a teacher or parent go through the searching process by using a personal topic allows them to easily come up with the questions, search terms, and evaluation criteria for the information on the Web sites they locate. They are often interested in online information about pets and hobbies such as quilting, cross-stitch, and surf fishing, as well as areas related to their work, such as desktop publishing, photography, cabinetry, and nursing. However, once I shift the emphasis to a topic they are unfamiliar with, they have difficulty with the process. It is immediately evident to them how important it is students have a thorough knowledge-base in the content before beginning to formulate the research question and gather and evaluate data. They realize that information literacy skills should not be taught in a vacuum, but as an integral, integrated, and important part of classroom content.

Information literacy skills should not be taught in a vacuum.

THE QUESTIONING PROCESS

With the enormous amount of information available, both in print and on the Web, students now more than ever need to define their topics very carefully before beginning a

Web-based search. A broad topic such as "farming in the 1930s" will retrieve huge amounts of information; "the effect of the Dust Bowl on migration patterns in the United States" will present the student with a manageable amount of information from a search. Identification of keywords, synonyms, and search strategies should be done before going out on the Web.

Many Web sites themselves provide information literacy models that focus on the questioning process as the basis for research. These include

From Now On: The Research Cycle at http://www.questioning.org/rcycle.html

The Big6 Information Problem-Solving Approach at http://big6.com

Info Zone Research Skills at http://www.pembinatrails.ca/infozone/

THE SEARCHING PROCESS

If library media specialists were organizing the information on the Web, it would all be catalogued using a thesaurus of terms and would be as easy to use as your local library card catalogue. Unfortunately, this is not the case. Searching for information on the Web differs from search tool to search tool. Students should be directed to first read the help files in the search engine or directory they choose to use. The help files include instructions for the creation of the queries and also give helpful tips and tricks for use of that particular search tool. One tip is to use the advanced search page of any online tool, which allows students to narrow their search by eliminating unnecessary words, by date, or by type of information.

Here are some useful search tutorials:

Recommended Search Strategies: Search with Peripheral Vision at
http://www.lib.berkeley.edu/TeachingLib/Guides/Internet/Strategies.html
Choose the Best Search Engine for Your Information Needs at
http://www.noodletools.com/debbie/literacies/information/5locate/adviceengine.html
Finding it Online: Web Search Strategies at
http://www.learnwebskills.com/search/main.html

THE EVALUATION PROCESS

The sheer amount of information found on the Web makes the skill of critical evaluation of information even more critical to information literacy than ever before. Information can be published by anyone on the Web, without any editorial or expert review. The ease of use of Web page creation tools can also make information look very credible when in fact it is totally untrue.

> Web information can look very credible when in fact it is totally untrue.

Five questions students can ask themselves when reviewing information found on the Web include

- Who wrote the pages and is the author an expert in the field?

- What does the author say is the purpose of the site?

- When was the site created, updated, or last worked on?

- Where does the information come from?

- Why is the information useful?

There are many informative sites on the Web dealing with the critical evaluation of information at all levels and tips and tricks to determine the validity of a site. A collection of these online tools and articles may be found at http://discoveryschool.com/schrock-guide/eval.html.

One fun activity for students is to critically evaluate a totally bogus site. Here are two excellent sites for this exercise:

Feline Reactions to Bearded Men at http://www.improb.com/airchives/classical/cat/cat.html

Critical evaluation of information can only be done properly once the student has a knowledge base in the topic. This is still best obtained through traditional print reference materials. Until the students know a little bit about the topic, it is difficult for

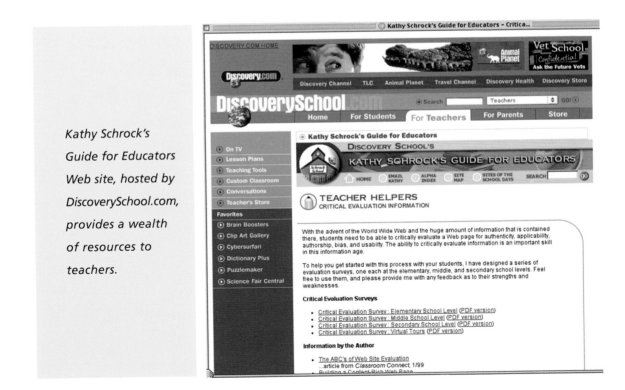

Kathy Schrock's Guide for Educators Web site, hosted by DiscoverySchool.com, provides a wealth of resources to teachers.

them to evaluate whether the online information they find is credible or valid. Another fun exercise for students to easily see that there is incorrect information on the Web is to view pages dealing with topics in which they do have a knowledge base, such as sports, music, Pokemon, movies, cars, video games, and the like. They soon find some incorrect posted information and realize that information on the Web cannot be taken at face value.

> **Students soon find some incorrect posted information and realize that information on the Web cannot be taken at face value.**

THE CITATION PROCESS

Bibliographic citations are more important than ever for Web-based information. First, citations allow students to easily revisit a resource they find to support their research. Second, citations allow educators to verify that the information handed in by students was not simply cut and pasted from a Web site. The Napster controversy has publicized the concept of intellectual property, and students should be knowledgeable about respecting intellectual property rights. Students should learn to ask permission to use others' information in a presentation or paper, as well as completing the correct citation format for electronic information used. Here are some sites to help with these skills:

NoodleBib tools at http://www.noodletools.com/tools.html

Student Permission to Use Web Resources for a Project at http://www.landmark-project.com/permission1.php

Related Web site: school.discovery.com/schrockguide

TAPPED IN

Connecting Communities of Learners

TERRIE GRAY

In 1997, I developed a Web site called ED's Oasis, funded by AT&T's Learning Network, to help teachers use the Internet as an integral tool for teaching and learning. Two objectives—to help teachers know where to go on the Internet and to help teachers know what to do with online materials—resulted in the creation of a set of Web site evaluation guidelines and three kinds of resources: links to the best educational Web sites, stories of teaching experiences, and a library of Internet-based lesson plans.

> Just interacting online doesn't automatically mean people are learning from one another.

From the beginning, Oasis staff wanted to provide more than just resources. We believed teachers would derive greater benefit if ED's Oasis was an online learning community. And we knew that just having people interact online did not automatically mean they were learning from one another.

During our first year we tried several online strategies (discussion boards, e-mail lists, surveys, and the like) to increase the level of participation by visitors to ED's Oasis, but we were unable to bring folks together into a cohesive community.

TAPPING IN TO TAPPED IN

Then we discovered TAPPED IN, a thriving "community of communities" developed by SRI International to meet informal networking and formal professional growth needs of K–12 teachers. At first glance, TAPPED IN looks like a chat room, but it provides more than just text-based communication in a real-time mode. Using the metaphor of a building, TAPPED IN provides a graphical Web interface that allows participants to come together in "rooms" for such purposes as communicating with each other, looking at Web sites together, and creating documents together. And unlike other online settings, TAPPED IN doesn't allow participants to be anonymous or to profess to be someone they are not. A searchable profile must be provided by all participants and verified by TAPPED IN staff.

Educators can come together in special user groups devoted to teaching in the K–3 primary grades, high school science, the arts, foreign language, or social studies. Teachers from Indiana, Pennsylvania, and California have connected their high school students for an online forum on civil rights. In a foreign language project, American high school students discussed Kosovo with middle-school students from France—in Spanish!

Tools for saving and sharing documents created online are available and easy to use. A transcript of the whole electronic conversation is made and can be e-mailed to participants after their TAPPED IN session. Early text-based chat sessions provided the initial step in online collaboration. TAPPED IN has taken a large leap by creating a comprehensive graphical interface that allows real use of online tools for a variety of purposes by a number of participants simultaneously.

THE POWER OF HAVING SOMEONE TO TALK TO

In TAPPED IN, the human infrastructure is the critical element. TAPPED IN is staffed by helpful education professionals and populated by teachers from across the country. There are now nearly fourteen thousand TAPPED IN users, including teachers, media librarians, administrators, technology coordinators, and education professors and graduate students. This means that it is easy to reach a critical mass of participants; there is usually someone to talk to. Nothing is more deadly to an online community than the "empty house" syndrome. Conversation is pointless when you're the only one present. ED's Oasis used the TAPPED IN environment in both formal and informal ways. It is where we held staff meetings, had regular office hours, led tours of ED's Oasis, and helped teachers find instructional materials.

> The human infrastructure is the critical element.

For example, we used TAPPED IN to prepare for the first MasterSearch Internet lesson plan contest. We hoped to build an online library of exemplary lessons as well as honor the teachers who developed them. Through TAPPED IN, we met and debated what a good lesson plan looked like—for example, we wanted to make sure the plans were student-centered, used the Internet in powerful ways, were standards-based, and had assessment built in. Because our judging staff was drawn from across the United States and Canada, it was financially impossible to judge contest entries as a group in a single physical location. Instead, we used our offices in TAPPED IN. We practiced judging by examining a Web page version of a sample entry in one browser window, and we "talked" to each other in another as we went through the scoring rubric step-by -step. We were able to clarify ambiguities in the wording of the rubric and refine the contest judging process.

HONORING MASTER TEACHERS THROUGH ONLINE SHARING

Another successful use of TAPPED IN has been to honor our MasterSearch winners by featuring them as guests in special online meetings. It is not uncommon for contest winners or Teachers of the Year to be celebrated at conferences where they shine in a brief public spotlight. But it is unusual for them to be available to other teachers and to share their strategies and experiences with educators around the world in a single session. Using TAPPED IN, we hosted online events during which MasterSearch contest winners presented their winning lessons, responded to questions, and shared Web page examples of student work. This type of activity is the work of a learning community. Participants who might not ordinarily even meet each other learn from the shared experiences of others. (MasterSearch contests still take place, and the library of lessons, as well as information about the contest, can be found at http://www.classroomconnect.com.)

ED's Oasis is now hosted by Classroom Connect, where resources available to teachers have been greatly expanded. Online opportunities for building communities are growing. TAPPED IN provided a model for what was possible in collaboration using the Internet. It continues to evolve new features using the latest technology for online communities. Over the years, the experiences of teachers, students, professors, and program directors have demonstrated that TAPPED IN works and still provides the right conditions for the development of a powerful online educational learning community.

Relationships forged in TAPPED IN sessions are enduring. Relationships built online have laid the groundwork for collegiality at conferences and other face-to-face meetings and have transcended geography, time, and job changes. Since the community of educational technology experts is small but growing, it's been even more important to maintain the contact with others made possible by TAPPED IN—for inspiration, encouragement, and renewal.

Related Web site: www.tappedin.org

Leadership Development

Professionals in medicine, architecture, finance, and law pursue ongoing opportunities to develop their skill levels and meet criteria for certifying their professional advancement. Similarly, leading teachers and school administrators are also engaged in demanding forms of professional development to develop their skills as instructional leaders.

Leadership opportunities for educators are important for enhancing professional skills and renewing personal commitment, and for creating a network of colleagues with shared experience. Creating these cadres of leaders can translate directly into improved teaching and learning in classrooms.

This section begins with the paths of two teachers in achieving National Board certification, the highest and most rigorous level of certification in the teaching profession. Other articles describe a training program for the principalship, which requires additional skills of teachers who move into the position, as well as one superintendent who is providing leadership in educational technology and creating a "digital district."

What parents can do:

- Through the PTA and other organizations, promote the concept of leadership development in your school and district to encourage lead teachers, principals, and other administrators to engage in such activities.

What educators can do:

- Support leadership development in schools and districts, viewing all educators as lifelong learners.

- Advocate for funds and programs to support the development of lead teachers, principals, school board members, superintendents, and other administrators.

- Document the benefits of professional development for these groups.

What policymakers can do:

- Become familiar with programs that provide professional development for principals, superintendents, and school board members, as well as the continued development of the best teachers.

- Support policies and funding that promote the development of educational leaders at school sites and in districts and states.

38

Becoming an Accomplished Teacher in the Twenty-First Century

DAVE FORREST AND MARILYN FORREST

Teaching, like other professions, now has national standards for professional achievement and a process for certifying its leading practitioners. Since 1995, more than 9,500 teachers have been awarded National Board Certification, which honors the highest level of professional teaching excellence, based on submission of student work samples, videotapes of classroom teaching, and rigorous analyses of the candidate's teaching and resulting student learning.

Dave and Marilyn Forrest, husband-and-wife teachers at James Logan High School in Union City, California, achieved Board Certification in 1999 after more than four hundred hours of preparation and almost two hundred pages of written work. Dave, a history teacher, and Marilyn, an English teacher, each received a $10,000 stipend from the State of California for becoming National Board Certified teachers. In this article, the Forrests tell how integration of technology into their respective curricula played an important role in demonstrating their teaching skills.—Eds.

After teaching high school history and English for many years at James Logan High School, we decided to accept the challenge of becoming National Board Certified teachers. During the intense, yearlong journey to demonstrate we were accomplished teachers, we videotaped our classrooms, compiled a portfolio of our classroom practices, documented our contact with parents and our professional colleagues, and took four rigorous written tests in our certification area. Throughout the process, instructional technology played an important role in helping us meet the challenges of certification.

> Instructional technology played an important role in helping us meet the challenges of certification.

The National Board for Professional Teaching Standards (NBPTS), formed over a decade ago, aims "to establish high and rigorous standards for what accomplished teachers should know and be able to do; [and] to develop and operate a national, voluntary system to assess and certify teachers who meet these standards." The National Board is unique because all of the assessments are developed by teachers, and only practicing teachers are involved in the scoring of the assessments.

TECHNOLOGY SUPPORTS NATIONAL BOARD CERTIFICATION

Although NBPTS standards do not require certified teachers to demonstrate proficiency in the use of computers with their students, classroom computer use was an important component of the accomplished teaching we demonstrated to achieve certification.

For example, as part of the social science-history certification, Dave needed to show that his history students were making real-world connections between the past and the communities they live in today. Dave had his students create an Internet publishing project called "History Close to Home." In this project, students wrote an interview of a person who lived through an important historical event. Once students completed their historical research and wrote their interviews, they published their stories on the Internet.

Publishing their interviews on the Internet proved to be a powerful experience for Dave's students. They worked hard to write well because they were writing for a real audience, and the project incorporated valuable skills. Each student learned how to create a Web page, take a digital photo, scan a picture, and design original digital artwork. Most important, this project brought history to life by documenting the stories of parents who had fought in wars, relatives who had escaped persecution in other countries, and senior citizens who had lived during the Great Depression.

> Students worked hard to write well because they were writing for a real audience.

CONNECTION TO THE COMMUNITY

The History Close to Home project also helped Dave demonstrate outreach to students' families and the community, a requirement for National Board Certification. For example, Dave received an e-mail note from one student's mother that said, "Erika loves your class. . . . My family is excited about the Web site. My brother and sister are waiting patiently for it to be completed so they can visit it. My mother, who is computer-shy, plans to go over to a friend's house to see it." In addition, Dave created a classroom Web page with daily classroom assignments linked to Internet resources to help students with those assignments. Parents appreciated being able to use this Internet page to follow the progress of their student's class.

The use of technology in Marilyn's English class helped her fulfill the "Student Response to Text" portfolio requirement. Teachers are asked to show how they use non-print text or media to help teach reading. Marilyn exposes her students to a variety of literature and other media to help them make connections among different forms of writing and across content areas. She wants them to become engaged emotionally in what they read and learn to have empathy for others, even in an imagined setting. A computer program

Marilyn developed on John Steinbeck's 1930s-era novel, *Of Mice and Men*, asks students to examine and respond to Dorothea Lange photographs from the Depression prior to reading the novel. One entry in her portfolio is a student poem called "Lonely in Poverty." The poem, written in response to the lesson, demonstrates the student's emotional engagement with the pictures and readiness to start reading the novel.

One aspect of accomplished teaching, according to the National Board, is contributing to the improvement of the teaching profession as a whole. Marilyn's design of several computer-based multimedia curricula helped her achieve a high score in the "Documented Accomplishments" area of her portfolio. She demonstrated how technology should not be a skill taught in isolation but one integrated into the content areas. These curricula supplement the teaching of reading and writing skills for the core works taught in ninth and tenth grades. She has encouraged and trained other teachers to use the computers they have in their classrooms by sharing the lessons she has developed.

In November 1999, we received the good news that both of us had achieved National Board Certification. The road to becoming nationally board-certified teachers was often difficult, but achieving certification provided a real sense of accomplishment and validation in a profession that often comes with few rewards. The National Board Certification process is a beginning toward raising the bar we set for all of our nation's teachers.

Our belief is that being an accomplished teacher in the twenty-first century must include the thoughtful integration of technology into classroom instruction. Our hope is that helping students learn to use powerful computer tools will become an expectation for all teachers, and a hallmark of our most accomplished ones.

Related Web site: www.nbpts.org

North Carolina Principals Go Back to School

"The principalship is the loneliest occupation I've ever had."

The words of North Carolina elementary school principal Mike Chappell echo the sentiments of many in the leadership position at our nation's ninety-one thousand public school sites. "As a teacher, even as an assistant principal, I always felt there was someone I could talk to, brainstorm with, commiserate with," says Chappell. "But when you become principal, you're on your own."

> When you become principal, you're on your own.

When he heard about a professional development program that would enable him to share ideas with principals throughout the state, Chappell jumped at the opportunity to participate. Five times in one year he traveled to Chapel Hill, where he spent three days on the University of North Carolina campus. There he participated in the Higher School

263

Performance Program, one of several professional development courses offered through the Principals' Executive Program (PEP) at UNC's Center for School Leadership.

During each of the UNC sessions, Chappell and his colleagues from throughout North Carolina participated in intensive seminars addressing a range of issues facing public school principals. They wrestled with test score data, studied curriculum development, brainstormed ways to improve parent involvement, discussed standards-based instruction, and explored such critical issues as student conduct, instructional monitoring, and teacher support and supervision.

"It was just the right mix of theory and practical application," says Chappell, who continues to draw on the skills and lessons learned at PEP.

PRINCIPALS DIGGING INTO SCHOOL DATA

At a time when the right test scores can mean monetary rewards and the wrong ones can mean state takeovers, it's no surprise that Chappell and others found the program's emphasis on data analysis particularly valuable.

Principals arrive at UNC with test results for their own schools in hand, so their data are not fictitious and their analyses are not abstract. The numbers are real—and subsequent corrective measures are specific to their school and their students.

"Numbers don't have any meaning in and of themselves," says Chappell. "You have to dig deep to understand what's behind the data."

And dig deep is exactly what he had his own teaching staff do. At a series of off-campus, grade-level retreats, Zebulon Elementary School teachers immersed themselves in stu-

> The right test scores can mean monetary rewards and the wrong ones can mean state takeovers.

dent test data, analyzing trends, identifying areas for further study and—ultimately—developing grade-by-grade action plans for improving student achievement.

Because of those sessions, says Chappell, his staff identified a need to strengthen the program for academically gifted students and to improve coordination between classroom teachers and the school's special education and resource teachers.

"Those sessions allowed everyone to become stakeholders in the process," says Chappell. "Everyone needs to be ready to take up the torch when you pass it to them."

"EACH SESSION WAS LIKE A CHRISTMAS GIFT"

As first-year principals of a newly opened charter school, Phyllis Brown and Patricia Edge were apprehensive about being away from school for three days for their first of five Higher School Performance Program seminars. "It was a major thing to be away from school for three days at the beginning of the school year," says Brown. "We just kept saying to ourselves, 'This had better be worth it.'"

It didn't take long, however, before Brown and Edge realized that the days spent on the UNC campus would have a profound impact on them and on the organization of their new school. "Each session was like a Christmas gift opened up in front of us," recalls Brown, adding that because of the information learned at PEP, she and Edge worked with their staff to revamp their class schedule.

"The speakers were phenomenal," says Brown, noting that their comments addressed the practical—handling discipline problems, creating class schedules and the like—and the motivational, as principals shared stories about their own struggles and successes. "I remember one principal in particular who was my absolute favorite," says Brown. "She talked about arriving at a school 'in shambles,' and about the little things she did each day to bring her school up—things we could do at our own schools."

CREATING HOPE, FOSTERING CHANGE

For Shirley Arrington, director of the Higher School Performance Program, it's vital that principals understand the many complex factors that contribute to the "achievement gap" in many of our nation's schools. She and her colleague Gene Gallelli work together to plan topics that will address the complex issues facing today's principals, while challenging them to create a new vision for their schools and their communities.

"Many of us are in schools with poor and minority children and we're operating from a middle-class or upper-middle-class perspective," says Arrington. "We need to spend less time blaming kids and blaming parents, less time saying, `ain't it awful,' and more time figuring out what we can do in our buildings to motivate teachers and engage parents."

To that end, the strategies, the skills, and the motivational speakers all share a common purpose: to help principals get beyond their day-to-day problems and begin exploring how they can stimulate change in their school communities.

"The principal has an incredible impact on the behavior of teachers and parents," says Arrington. "They need to be optimistic and they need to be willing to challenge others to acknowledge problems and move on."

Thanks to the Higher School Performance program, say Chappell and Brown, they're able to do just that.

The Digital Superintendent

Selling the Vision to Parents, Teachers, and Voters

WILLIAM SNIDER

Doug Otto remembers when he bought his first personal computer in Davenport, Iowa—an Apple Macintosh, shortly after the Mac made its splashy debut in 1984. He liked its "graphical user interface," which didn't require learning obscure commands to use it. Otto, who had just launched his career as a school superintendent, starting out by crafting professional meeting agendas and writing memos to his school board on its small black-and-white screen.

At the time, visionary educators were just starting to figure out how to integrate technology into the classroom. "It seemed most important to get students familiar with technology as a separate subject," recalls Otto. "All kids needed to learn keyboarding and programming. Programming, in turn, could help teach logic and math. I spread that vision everywhere I went in the district. Little did I know how much more meaningful technology would become."

Over the years, Otto refined his vision for educational technology and led innovations in a number of school districts as his career progressed. Today, he leads one of the most wired school districts in the nation—Plano Independent School District (ISD), a suburban district north of Dallas with fifty-nine schools and close to forty-nine thousand students, 30 percent of whom are Asian American, Hispanic, or black. Under his leadership, Plano ISD has adopted technologies ranging from a fiber-optic network to handheld personal digital assistants (PDAs). Technology is so integral to the district's education program that "we can't teach the curriculum without it," says Otto.

THE POWER OF LIGHT

The "information superhighway" is often more like a winding country road.

The Internet is sometimes called the "information superhighway" but, when accessed via a dial-up connection, it's often no faster than a winding country road. Plano ISD has a true superhighway: a state-of-the-art fiber-optic network inaugurated in September 2001 through a partnership with Southwestern Bell. The fiber-optic network can transfer information—converted to pulses of light—at 2,488 megabits per second, or over sixteen hundred times the capacity of Plano ISD's previous network.

The twenty-three thousand computers in Plano ISD's sixty-six school and administration buildings are linked by nearly a hundred miles of fiber-optic cable. The network allows students and teachers to view a central library of more than a thousand digital videos, access online curriculum, conduct videoconferences with other classrooms or communities, and exploit the Internet fully from every classroom.

On a smaller scale, the district is experimenting with the use of handheld personal digital assistants (PDAs) to see if putting the latest technology right in students' hands will open up more avenues for learning. High school students are using the handheld devices to learn essential life skills such as goal setting, time management, team building, and money management. First graders are using them—with an attached keyboard to accommodate their developing hand-eye coordination and fine motor skills—to work individually with math software and beam add-on stories to each other. The handheld devices are also a promising new way for parents and teachers to coordinate a child's activities, in terms not only of schedules but also of learning goals. The results are not yet in, but Otto sees handheld devices "as the only way get to a one-to-one computing ratio—we just can't afford to equip all students with a computer."

> **Handheld devices are the only way get to a one-to-one computing ratio.**

In another pilot, administrators at one school are using the handheld devices to improve security and keep better track of students' whereabouts. The devices carry information about each student's schedule, address, phone number, and parent contact information, which can be accessed manually or by scanning a bar code on student ID badges.

VISION FROM THE TOP

Otto is convinced that disseminating a technology vision for his district is a vital part of his leadership position. "A lot of people have energy, enthusiasm, and good ideas for integrating technology into learning," he says. "But you'll never get total, meaningful implementation unless there is a vision from the top that everyone can look at and buy into and hopefully implement at the classroom level."

"The skills that students acquire doing research, analyzing, and synthesizing and presenting information will stay with them for life," Otto contends. "The world is much more reliant on information and technology, and having the skills to research and present information is critical."

In addition, technology allows teaching and learning to keep pace with the evolving body of human knowledge. "The Pythagorean Theorem is still the same today as it was a hundred years ago, but math books cost $60 and wear out very quickly," says Otto. "When you turn to areas such as social studies and science, things are constantly changing. Technology provides access to totally up-to-date information—if the student chooses. There is no other tool that allows them to do that."

Otto's vision and salesmanship help to explain why, over the past decade, voters have approved a series of bond initiatives for Plano ISD's extraordinary technology infrastructure. In a Republican-dominated school district, the bond measures have been passing by a better than 3:1 margin.

In 1999, voters approved spending $14.6 million on new technologies such as the fiber-optic network. But new technology is a relatively easy sell—more impressive has been the voters' willingness to approve bonds for more mundane things like replacing PCs according to a set schedule. "We find it is more cost-effective to replace equipment and always buy computers with four-year warranties," says Otto. "That way, we don't pay a dime to repair computers or maintain a repair staff."

"When you depend on technology like we do, if our downtime is just 1 percent, we can't deliver curriculum to somebody," he adds. "We try to keep our downtime to zero."

> The skills that students acquire doing research, analyzing, and synthesizing and presenting information will stay with them for life.

A MOBILE SUPERINTENDENT STAYS IN TOUCH

With all the technology at their disposal, Plano ISD administrators can manage their district with the same tools available to their counterparts in private businesses. Technology has brought new efficiencies throughout the district, from hiring and procurement to scheduling and record keeping. Perhaps nowhere is the impact of new technology more apparent than in the area of communication.

The Plano ISD Web site and e-mail messages have become the preferred way for the district to communicate with parents—and vice versa. When administrators make a decision, "we get instant feedback," says Otto. "People can tell us what they think right away—they don't have to write a letter or pick up the phone."

Technology has brought new efficiencies throughout the district.

Some parents feel that Plano ISD has gone too far in embracing technology at the expense of more traditional teaching and learning. But their most visible means of rallying supporters to the cause is a technologically sophisticated "unofficial" Web site that rivals the district's own. It would be hard to argue with the district's success as measured by achievement tests. In the spring of 2001, Plano students continued to outperform students from across the state on the Texas Assessment of Academic Skills. Scores at every grade level remained above the Texas "exemplary" standard. Nationally, SAT scores of Plano students are among the highest for districts with more than twenty thousand students (in 2000, a combined verbal and math average of 1,122 compared with a national average of 1,019). At the same time, Plano's music education program has been voted one of the best in the nation for two years running.

Otto finds himself fielding fifty or more e-mail messages each day, often via the handheld PDA he carries everywhere he goes. "I spend a lot more time communicating with parents and staff members," he says. "I don't know if that is good or bad. The negative is I can never get away from the job. But people want to keep informed, they want to have contact with the superintendent or their principal. So the technology is positive because it helps us fulfill the expectations of the community."

Superintendent Doug Otto.

RESOURCES

PART 1. INNOVATIVE CLASSROOMS

A   PROJECT-BASED LEARNING

Barre, D., Hardy, J., and Harper, D. *Generation www.Y Curriculum Kit* (2nd ed.). Eugene, Oreg.: ISTE, 2001.

Berger, R. *A Culture of Quality: A Reflection on Practice.* Providence, R.I.: Annenberg Institute for School Reform, 1996.

"Block Scheduling." University of Minnesota. http://education.umn.edu/carei/Blockscheduling/default.html

Carter, K. "Laptop Lessons: Exploring the Promise of One-to-One Computing." http://www.techlearning.com/db_area/archives/TL/200105/laptops.html

Chard, S. *The Project Approach: Making the Curriculum Come Alive.* New York: Scholastic, 1998.

"Class-Size Reduction Program." http://www.ed.gov/offices/OESE/ClassSize

Exploratorium. *Hands-On Science: A Teacher's Guide to Student-Built Experiments and the Exploratorium Science Snackbook.* San Francisco: Exploratorium, 1991. http://www.exploratorium.edu/snacks/Hands-On_Science

Forsten, C., Grant, J., and Richardson, I. "Multiage and Looping: Borrowing from the Past." Alexandria, Va.: National Association of Elementary School Principals, March 1999.

Gardner, H. *Intelligence Reframed: Multiple Intelligences for the Twenty-First Century.* New York: Basic Books, 2000.

Gordon, D. (ed.). *The Digital Classroom: How Technology Is Changing the Way We Teach and Learn.* Cambridge, Mass.: Harvard Education Letter, 2000.

Katz, L. G., and Chard, S. C. *Engaging Children's Minds: The Project Approach* (2nd ed.). Norwood, N.J.: Ablex, 2000.

Lowther, D., and Morrison, G. *Integrating Computer Technology Into the Classroom.* Upper Saddle River, N.J.: Prentice Hall, 2001.

National Foundation for the Improvement of Education. *Connecting the Bits: A Reference for Using Technology in Teaching and Learning in K-12 Schools.* Washington, D.C.: National Foundation for the Improvement of Education, 2000.

Thomas, J. W., Mergendoller, J. R., and Michaelson, A. *Project Based Learning: A Handbook for Middle and High School Teachers.* Novato, Calif.: Buck Institute for Education, 1999.

B   SOCIAL/EMOTIONAL LEARNING

Cohen, J. (ed.). *Educating Minds and Hearts: Social Emotional Learning and the Passage into Adolescence.* Alexandria, Va.: Association for Supervision and Curriculum Development, 1999.

Collaborative for Academic, Social and Emotional Learning (CASEL). http://www.casel.org

Elias, M., and others. *Promoting Social and Emotional Learning: Guidelines for Educators.* Alexandria, Va.: Association for Supervision and Curriculum Development, 1997.

Elias, M., and Tobias, S. *Emotionally Intelligent Parenting.* New York: Random House, 1999.

Elias, M. J., Friedlander, B. S., and Tobias, S. E. *Engaging the Resistant Child Through Computers: A Manual to Facilitate Social and Emotional Learning.* Port Chester, N.Y.: Dude, 2001.

Goleman, D. *Emotional Intelligence: Why It Can Matter More Than IQ.* New York: Bantam, 1995.

Gordon, T. *Parent Effectiveness Training: The Proven Program for Raising Responsible Children, Thirtieth Anniversary Edition.* New York: Three Rivers Press, 2000.

Lantieri, L., and Patti, J. *Waging Peace in Our Schools.* Boston: Beacon Press, 1996.

C   ASSESSMENT

Bernhardt, V. L. *The School Portfolio Toolkit.* Larchmont, N.Y.: Eye on Education, 2002.

Darling-Hammond, L., and Ancess, J. *Authentic Assessment in Action.* New York: Teachers College Press, 1995.

Means, B., Penuel, W. R., and Padilla, C. *The Connected School: Technology and Learning in High School.* New York: Wiley, 2001.

Moskal, B. M. "Scoring Rubrics: What, When, and How." ERIC Clearinghouse on Assessment and Evaluation and the Department of Measurement, Statistics, and Evaluation, University of Maryland, College Park. http://www.ericdigests.org/2001-2/scoring.html

National Center for Research on Evaluations, Standards, and Student Testing (CRESST). http://cresst96.cse.ucla.edu

Pellegrino, J. W., Chudowsky, N., and Glaser, R. (eds.). *Knowing What Students Know: The Science and Design of Educational Assessment.* Washington, D.C.: National Academy Press, 2001.

Phillips, S. E. *Legal Implications of High-Stakes Assessment: What States Should Know.* North Central Regional Educational Laboratory (NCREL).

Practical Assessment, Research & Evaluation (PARE). ERIC Clearinghouse on Assessment and Evaluation and the Department of Measurement, Statistics, and Evaluation, University of Maryland, College Park. http://pareonline.net/

Stiggins, R. *Student-Involved Assessment* (3rd ed.). Upper Saddle River, N.J.: Prentice Hall, 2001.

Wiggins, G. *Educative Assessment: Designing Assessments to Inform and Improve Student Performance.* San Francisco: Jossey-Bass, 1998.

Wiggins, G., and McTighe, J. *Understanding by Design.* Alexandria, Va.: Association for Supervision and Curriculum Development, 1998.

PART 2: INVOLVED COMMUNITIES

A   PARENT INVOLVEMENT

National PTA. *Building Successful Partnerships: A Guide for Developing Parent and Family Involvement Programs.* Bloomington, Ind.: National Educational Services, 2000.

National PTA. Available online: http://pta.org

B　　BUSINESS PARTNERSHIPS

National Academy Foundation. http://naf.org

Business Roundtable. http://www.businessroundtable.org

National Career Academy Coalition. http://www.ncacinc.org

National Association of Partners in Education. http://www.napehq.org

Walsh, M. "Business Leaders Urged to Step Up Support for Schools." *Education Week,* April 1998.

C　　COMMUNITY PARTNERSHIPS

Berman, S. "Service Learning as Systemic Reform," 2000. http://www.hudson.k12.ma.us/publications/csl.htm

Cummins, J., and Sayers, D. *Brave New Schools: Challenging Cultural Illiteracy Through Global Learning Networks.* New York: St. Martin's Press, 1995.

National Coalition for Parent Involvement in Education. http://www.ncpie.org

Partnership for Family Involvement in Education. http://www.ed.gov/pubs/whoweare/index.html

R*TEC (Regional Technology in Education Consortium). http://www.rtec.org/

U.S. Department of Education. *Schools as Centers of Community: A Citizen's Guide for Planning and Design.* April 2000. http://www.ed.gov/offices/OESE/archives/inits/construction/commguide.pdf

PART 3: SKILLFUL EDUCATORS

A　　TEACHER PREPARATION

American Federation of Teachers. Available online: http://www.aft.org

Clark, R. *Effective Professional Development Schools.* San Francisco: Jossey-Bass, 1999.

Darling-Hammond, L. *The Right to Learn: A Blueprint for Creating Schools That Work.* San Francisco: Jossey-Bass, 2001.

Darling-Hammond, L., and Sykes, G. *Teaching as the Learning Profession: Handbook of Policy and Practice.* San Francisco: Jossey-Bass, 1999.

Fideler, E., and Haselkorn, D. *Learning the Ropes: Urban Teacher Induction Programs and Practices in the United States.* Belmont, Mass.: Recruiting New Teachers, 1999.

Ladson-Billings, G. *Crossing Over to Canaan: The Journey of New Teachers in Diverse Classrooms.* San Francisco: Jossey-Bass, 2001.

National Coalition for Technology in Education and Training. http://nctet.org

National Council for Accreditation of Teacher Education. http://ncate.org

Wisniewski, R., "Re-Creating Colleges of Teacher Education." http://www.bellsouthfoundation.org/pdfs/slnreport.pdf

B   ONGOING PROFESSIONAL DEVELOPMENT

American Federation of Teachers. http://www.aft.org

From Now On. http://fno.org

International Society for Technology in Education. http://www.iste.org

Kathy Schrock's Guide for Educators. http://school.discovery.com/schrockguide

McKenzie, J. *Beyond Technology: Questioning, Research and the Information Literate School.* Bellingham, Wash.: FNO Press, 2000.

Mecca, A. M. *The Mentoring Revolution: Growing America One Child at a Time— Part I.* Tiburon, Calif.: California Mentor Foundation, 2001.

National Education Association. http://www.nea.org

National Staff Development Council. http://www.nsdc.org

International Society for Technology in Education. *National Educational Technology Standards for Students.* Eugene, Oreg.: International Society for Technology in Education, 2000.

Senge, P. (ed.). *Schools That Learn: A Fifth Discipline Fieldbook for Educators, Parents, and Everyone Who Cares About Education.* New York: Doubleday, 2000.

Schrock, K., and Frazel, M. *Inquiring Educators Want to Know: TeacherQuests for Today's Teachers.* Worthington, Ohio: Linworth, 2000.

C   LEADERSHIP DEVELOPMENT

American Association of School Administrators. http://www.aasa.org

Barth, R. *Learning by Heart.* San Francisco: Jossey-Bass, 2001.

Kronley, R. A., and Handley, C. "Inspiring Leadership: A Philanthropic Partnership for Professional Development of Superintendents." BellSouth Foundation. http:www.bellsouthfoundation.org

National Association of Elementary School Principals. http://www.naesp.org

National Association of Elementary School Principals. *Leading Learning Communities: Standards for What Principals Should Know and Be Able to Do.* Alexandria, Va.: National Association of Elementary School Principals, 2001.

National Association of Secondary School Principals. http://www.nassp.org

National Board for Professional Teaching Standards: http://www.nbpts.org

National School Boards Association. http://nsba.org

Ohler, J. (ed.). *Future Courses: A Compendium of Thought About Education, Technology, and the Future.* Bloomington, Ind.: TECHNOS Press, 2001.

Thornburg, D. *Brainstorms and Lightning Bolts: Thinking Skills for the Twenty-First Century.* Lake Barrington, Ill.: Thornburg Center, 2000. http://www.tcpd.org/Thornburg/Handouts/brainstorms.pdf

GENERAL RESOURCES:

Bransford, J. D., Brown, A. L., and Cocking, R. R. (eds.). *How People Learn: Brain, Mind, Experience, and School.* Washington, D.C.: National Academy Press, 1999.

George Lucas Educational Foundation. *Learn & Live.* San Rafael, Calif.: George Lucas Educational Foundation, 1997.

Rockman et al (educational research). http://rockman.com

"The Building." http://www.newhorizons.org

THE EDITORS

MILTON CHEN, PH.D., is executive director of The George Lucas Educational Foundation. Dr. Chen serves on advisory boards for *Scholastic*, www.proquestk12.com, PBS, and Child Research Net in Japan. He has served as founding director of the KQED Center for Education & Lifelong Learning (PBS) in San Francisco, director of research at Sesame Workshop in New York, and assistant professor at the Harvard Graduate School of Education. He is a frequent speaker and media commentator on issues of education and the media.

SARA ARMSTRONG, PH.D., is director of content of The George Lucas Educational Foundation. Dr. Armstrong has been an educator for twenty-five years. Her classroom experience included integrating technology and telecommunications into the curriculum in the early 1980s. She serves on the National Storytelling Network's Board of Directors and is an associate of the Thornburg Center for Professional Development. She has been a presenter and keynote speaker at conferences nationwide, as well as at sessions in Seoul, Korea, and Curitiba, Brazil.

THE CONTRIBUTORS

Bruce Alberts, Ph.D., is president of the National Academy of Sciences and chair of the National Research Council. Dr. Alberts holds an American Cancer Society lifetime research professorship and is chair of the University of California, San Francisco (UCSF) department of biochemistry and biophysics. He is one of the principal authors of *The Molecular Biology of the Cell,* and most recently, *Essential Cell Biology.* He helped to create City Science, a program for improving science teaching in San Francisco elementary schools. Dr. Alberts received his doctorate from Harvard University.

Diane Curtis is a writer and editor at The George Lucas Educational Foundation. A long-time journalist, Ms. Curtis was an editorial writer and education reporter at the *San Francisco Chronicle.* She also reported for the Associated Press, the *Sacramento Bee,* the *San Jose Mercury News,* and United Press International.

Jorge Descamps, Ed.D., is co-director of the 1995 El Paso Technology Innovation Challenge Grant and professor of education at the University of Texas at El Paso.

Dave Forrest is a history teacher at Logan High School, Union City, California. Mr. Forrest achieved his National Board Certification from the National Board for Professional Teaching Standards in 1999. Mr. Forrest also has been teacher of the year, a mentor teacher, and a leader in integrating technology into the Logan High School curriculum. Mr. Forrest won the National Semi-Conductor Internet Innovator Award in 2000.

Marilyn Forrest is an English teacher at Logan High School, Union City, California. Ms. Forrest achieved her National Board Certification from the National Board for Professional Teaching Standards in 1999. Ms. Forrest also has been teacher of the year, a mentor teacher, and a leader in integrating technology into the Logan High School curriculum.

Roberta Furger is a writer at The George Lucas Educational Foundation. Ms. Furger is the author of *Does Jane Compute? Preserving Our Daughters' Place in the Cyber Revolution* (Warner Books, 1998) and a recipient of the 2001 San Francisco Women on the Web award.

John Gehring has been a staff writer at *Education Week* since 1999. Mr. Gehring covers higher education, school-to-work issues, and sports. He previously was a reporter for the *Frederick Gazette* and the *Catholic Review*. He received his master's in journalism from Columbia University. Mr. Gehring has won national journalism awards in sports writing and investigative reporting from the Catholic Press Association.

Milton Goldberg, Ph.D., is executive vice president of the National Alliance of Business. Dr. Goldberg previously served as head of the Office of Research in the U.S. Department of Education and was executive director of the commission that produced the landmark education report "A Nation at Risk." Dr. Goldberg is also a former high school teacher.

Daniel Goleman, Ph.D., is author of the 1995 international best-seller, *Emotional Intelligence.* In his book, Dr. Goleman cited a wealth of brain research to support the idea that such skills as self-control, getting along with others, perseverance, and self-motivation—emotional intelligence—may be more important than IQ in determining overall lifelong success. He also demonstrated that such skills can be taught, especially during childhood. He is also the author of *Working with Emotional Intelligence* and the coauthor of *Primal Leadership: Realizing the Power of Emotional Intelligence.*

Edwin H. Gragert, Ph.D., is director of iEARN-USA. Dr. Gragert's interest in international education began when he was seventeen and lived for a year in Asia as an exchange student. In his current position, he is able to apply his excitement for how technology enables people to work together and learn from each other in the service of improving our world.

Terrie Gray, Ed.D., is director of Connected University at Classroom Connect. Dr. Gray is the founder of ED's Oasis, a Web site that helps teachers use the Internet and links them to a variety of resources. In Dr. Gray's current position, she directs efforts that provide online professional development with challenging content and maximum interactivity. Dr. Gray received her Ed.D. from Pepperdine University.

George Lucas is chairman of the board of The George Lucas Educational Foundation. Mr. Lucas has long held a concern about how to improve education—a concern that focuses on heightening the vast imagination and curiosity of a child. Mr. Lucas grew up in the small town of Modesto, California, and attended the University of Southern California film school. As a storyteller, visionary, and innovator, his imagination reached into the galaxy with the *Star Wars* saga. Mr. Lucas is also creator of the *Indiana Jones* film series and the TV series *The Young Indiana Jones Chronicles.*

George E. Marsh II, Ed.D., is a professor in the Institute for Interactive Technology at the University of Alabama and an expert on technology in education. Dr. Marsh is a partner in emTech Consulting, both a Web site and a consulting firm that provides technology advice and resources to teachers. An author or coauthor of fifteen textbooks, he has developed software for education and business applications and has been a school administrator, psychometrist, and classroom teacher.

Anna C. McFadden, Ph.D., is an associate professor in the Institute for Interactive Technology at the University of Alabama and an expert on technology in education. Dr. McFadden has coauthored or contributed to eleven books and over twenty-five professional articles and is former editor of the *International Schools Services Sources/Internet Sources for Schools,* a journal for educators. She also is a partner in emTech Consulting, both a Web site and a consulting firm that provides technology advice and resources to teachers.

Ellen Moir is executive director of the New Teacher Center, University of California, Santa Cruz; director of teacher education, UCSC; and director of the Santa Cruz New Teacher Project. Ms. Moir has also produced a number of video documentaries on teacher induction and bilingual education, authored articles on teacher development, and regularly serves as a consultant and inspirational keynote speaker to school districts and educational organizations throughout the country.

Barrie Jo Price, Ed.D., is a professor in the Institute for Interactive Technology at the University of Alabama and an expert on technology in education. Dr. Price has coauthored fourteen books and twenty-six professional articles, participated in the development of almost two hundred pieces of commercial software, and worked with schools throughout the world. She is a partner in emTech Consulting, both a Web site and a consulting firm that provides technology advice and resources to teachers.

Cynthia Roberts is a freelance writer and editor. Ms. Roberts was founder and publisher of *Parents Express,* a monthly parenting newspaper in Philadelphia, and is a former editorial director of Totalwoman.com. She recently edited *Open the Doors, See All the People,* a guide to serving families in sacred buildings, published under a grant from the Annie E. Casey Foundation.

Mark Sargent is Web content manager at The George Lucas Educational Foundation. Mr. Sargent manages the Foundation's Web production and product development efforts. Prior to joining the Foundation, Mr. Sargent was the director at Putney Student Travel, a Vermont-based organization that designs and operates a variety of educational summer programs for high school students in the United States and overseas.

Kathy Schrock is an instructional technology specialist for a school district on Cape Cod, Massachusetts. Ms. Schrock is the creator of the popular site for teachers, Kathy Schrock's Guide for Educators, and has recently authored a book titled *Writing and Research on the Computer,* which provides teachers in grades 5–8 with the handouts necessary to implement the information literacy process in the classroom.

William Snider is a freelance writer and editor. Mr. Snider was the editor for *Learn & Live,* published by The George Lucas Educational Foundation in 1997, and former senior writer for *Education Week.* He has written about technology and education for more than fifteen years.

Lisa Wahl is an independent consultant. She has served as executive director of the Center for Accessible Technology in Berkeley, California.

Marilyn Wall is a fourth-grade teacher at Peak View Elementary School, Penn Laird, Virginia. Ms. Wall has been a teacher for over thirty years and has been honored as a

NASA Educator Workshop for Elementary Science Teachers Teacher, and as a National Science Teachers Association Teacher of the Year.

Cecelia Wambach, Ph.D., is a professor at San Francisco State University. Dr. Wambach was co-principal of John Muir Elementary School in San Francisco until 2001 as part of the Muir Alternative Teacher Education (MATE) program.

Virginia Watkins is principal of John Muir Elementary School in San Francisco, site of the Muir Alternative Teacher Education (MATE) program.

Grant Wiggins, Ed.D., is president and director of programs at Relearning by Design, a not-for-profit educational organization in Pennington, New Jersey. Dr. Wiggins earned his Ed.D. from Harvard University and his B.A. from St. John's College in Annapolis. He is the author of *Educative Assessment* and *Assessing Student Performance,* and coauthor with Jay McTighe of *Understanding by Design.*

This page constitutes a continuation of the copyright page.